# ANGKOR

*The Monuments of the God-Kings*

# CONTENTS

# ACKNOWLEDGMENTS

The ruins of Angkor have long fascinated me, and I have always felt that this vast and mysterious empire deserved to be shown photographed entirely in color. Finally I accomplished what I had dreamed of doing for so many years; this book documents the result.

I photographed Angkor just prior to Cambodia's involvement in the Indochinese conflict; since then, Angkor has been closed to visitors. I was thus one of the last fortunate enough to view these extraordinary monuments.

I wish to thank Miss So-Lan of Siem Reap, my tireless guide at Angkor. Roberta Hessdorfer, Donald Makepeace, Merrill Stickler, and Daniel Bourn gave their time and talent to making the prints, maps, and charts. And, most of all, I thank my wife, Edna, who accompanied me on this journey, climbed every rock, and recorded each click of the shutter.

BELA KALMAN

I wish to thank Professor John Rosenfield for his encouragement of this book and for his valuable comments on the manuscript. Wilma Fairbank, Piriya Krairiksh, Patricia M. Young, and Roberto Unger also read the text and made thoughtful suggestions, along with Thalia Kennedy Haak, who offered illuminating editorial ideas. Martine and Catherine Dean have aided with the French sources. The largest debt of thanks goes to my husband, whose loyalty compares with Rama's, resourcefulness with Hanuman's, and patience with Narayana's.

JOAN LEBOLD COHEN

# K

*Monu[...]*

*of the*

*God-[...]*

HARRY N. A[...]

IN MEMORY OF MILTON S. FOX

*Frontispiece.*   Portrait of Jayavarman VII. National Museum, Phnom-Penh

Nai Y. Chang, *Vice-President, Design and Production*
John L. Hochmann, *Executive Editor*
Margaret L. Kaplan, *Managing Editor*
Barbara Lyons, *Director, Photo Department, Rights and Reproductions*
Barbara Berg, *Editor*
Elaine Sherer Cox, *Designer*

Library of Congress Cataloging in Publication Data

Cohen, Joan Lebold.
    Angkor ; the monuments of the god-kings.

    Bibliography : p.
    1. Angkor, Cambodia. I. Title.
DS558.A6C586        915.96        72-6335
ISBN 0-8109-0075-0

Library of Congress Catalogue Card Number : 72-6335
Published by HARRY N. ABRAMS, INCORPORATED, NEW YORK, 1975.
All rights reserved. No part of the contents of this book may be
reproduced without the written permission of the publishers.
Printed and bound in Japan

G

HEN

# PREFACE

The Indochinese peninsula has been a meeting-ground for many cultures and the home of some intensely creative and inventive nations. The remarkable sculpture and architecture of ancient Cambodia is indisputable evidence of its brilliant cultural tradition. Because of the United States involvement in Southeast Asia in recent years, a far greater audience has become aware of the ancient civilization that once flourished there. The United States has tried to impose its values of democracy and industrial development on Southeast Asia with a zeal comparable to that of European missionaries who, beginning in the sixteenth century, tried to convert the "heathen idolators." This book will not explore the failures of both Christianity and democracy in Cambodia; its purpose is to examine the monuments of a society that succeeded so well in pursuing its own values from the sixth through the fifteenth centuries.

The earliest written record of the civilization which existed in the area we call Cambodia is found in a Chinese dynastic history of the third century of our era. Until the sixth century the Chinese called the country, which included the modern states of South Vietnam and southern Cambodia, "Funan." In the sixth century Funan was annexed by the neighboring state of Chenla, which had its power locus in the highlands of southern Laos and northern Cambodia. Chinese records show intermittent trade and tribute relations with Chenla (Cambodia) until modern times. The most complete eyewitness account was written by Chou Ta-kuan, an envoy from the Chinese court, who visited Chenla in 1296, approximately seventy-five years after the death of Jayavarman VII, the last great conqueror-builder of the Angkor period (ninth to fifteenth centuries). This was about eleven years after Marco Polo had touched the Indochinese shores (without seeing Angkor).

A few other early travelers to Asia—Arab seamen and Portuguese and Spanish missionaries—also mention the indigenous Khmer people of Cambodia and the sites on the Angkor plain which served as their capitals for six hundred years. Nevertheless, although Angkor was known to a few Westerners, it did not enter the body of Western learning until Henry Muhot's diary was published in French and English in the 1860s. A naturalist-explorer, Muhot had penetrated the Cambodian jungle during the period 1858–61 and had died there. His account, published posthumously, kindled the romantic imagination of nineteenth-century Europe and started a steady flow of visitors—scientists, scholars, sightseers, souvenir hunters, and robbers.

Popular interest in the ancient monuments was revived in the early 1920s when young André Malraux was imprisoned in Phnom Penh, charged with stealing sculptures from Banteay Srei. In 1930 he published his suspense-filled novel *The Royal Way*. In that book Malraux captured the mysterious essence of those majestic ruins with unmatched authenticity.

The Cambodia that was incorporated into French Indochina in the last half of the nineteenth century retained only cultural remnants of ancient Khmer grandeur. With the support of the French government, beginning in 1898, several generations of French scholars from the École Française d'Extrême-Orient diligently unraveled many of the mysteries of the Angkor civilization. They discovered, deciphered, preserved, and restored many of Cambodia's monuments.

The humid climate and the animal life of the jungle had destroyed Cambodia's perishable secrets—documents written on palm leaves or paper, and buildings and images made of wood. This left only stone structures with their carved decorations. After their discovery these sacred monuments, a brilliant, tangible expression of Khmer society, were studied from both archaeological and art-historical points of view. Explorations of the Indochinese peninsula and archipelago led to the discovery of some nine hundred stone tablets with inscriptions. Most of the Sanskrit and Khmer texts have been deciphered and, together with the previously mentioned Chinese dynastic histories and accounts of early travelers, have done much to explain the truly remarkable monuments of Angkor.

Although many scholarly works have contributed to our understanding, the author is particularly indebted to M. George Coedès for his brilliant evaluation of inscriptions and monuments and his depiction of the Khmer cultural context, especially in his volumes entitled *Angkor* and *The Indianized States of Southeast Asia*.

The present volume was conceived by the photographer Bela Kalman, who made a pilgrimage to photograph Angkor's monuments in March, 1970. Fortunately, it happened that his journey took place several days before the overthrow of Prince Sihanouk and the ensuing spread of the Indochinese conflict to Angkor itself.

J.L.C

# PART I
# EARLY ANGKOR

## and Its Origins

# Early Angkor and Its Origins

The grandeur of concept and brilliant execution of Angkor rank among man's highest achievements. A green cloak of silently encroaching jungle heightens the dramatic appearance of the buildings and sculpture, vestiges of a highly developed civilization that flourished between the ninth and fifteenth centuries A.D. To understand the significance of the monuments, we must look into the society that produced them.

Angkor was in large measure the product of Indian influences on the indigenous Khmer society. The people who inhabited Cambodia prior to the historic period were by no means primitive; they in fact possessed a somewhat sophisticated knowledge of bronze casting. The interaction between the indigenous society and the imported Indian culture resulted in the development of distinctive Khmer art forms, which emerged during the several centuries of building that preceded the first monuments shown in this book.

Indian culture had first reached Southeast Asia in the centuries before Christ, and gradually had become permanently woven into the overall pattern of the various Southeast Asian kingdoms. Except for the fact that this process was a peaceful one, the details are unclear. We do not know why the Indians came to Southeast Asia, but there can be no doubt that their ideas of religion, kingship, writing, and imagery accompanied them. Indian sacred texts written in Sanskrit brought the written word to what is now Cambodia, and eventually the spoken Khmer language was written down in a script adapted from those used in India. Through the long process of exposure to Indian culture, the Khmers came to view the world in Hindu and Buddhist terms. In distinctively Cambodian forms, they made and worshiped Indian gods who personify the unseen universal forces of creation and destruction; and they reproduced as their sacred buildings the vision of the Indian heavenly city as they perceived it.

The earliest powerful Indianized state in Southeast Asia, and the one to which the Khmers traced their heritage, was Funan, which in the period from the first to the sixth centuries gradually extended its domain along the coast and river deltas of South Vietnam and southern Cambodia, with its capital at Oc Eo. In a relationship similar to that of the countries bordering the Mediterranean, the Indianized kingdoms of Java and Sumatra vied with Funan for domination of the areas washed by the South China and Java Seas.

Early Indian leadership in the Funan community is reflected in an ancient tale of a Brahman priest who came to Cambodia and, after marrying a princess who was the daughter of the snake god, became king. The ruling dynasty of Funan supposedly derived from this sacred union. In the sixth century, according to another legend, a second Brahman came from India to save Funan from menacing neighbors. But the ruling dynasty was defeated, and Funan was incorporated into the adjoining state of Chenla, which was located in northern Cambodia and what is now the lower half of Laos. Two uneasy centuries of turmoil followed, and the state of Chenla split into two parts.

By the end of this period Chenla was forced into a tributary relationship with Java. According to the colorful tale of an eleventh-century Arab traveler, a haughty, short-lived prince of Chenla had expressed the Herod-like desire to see the Javanese king's head on a platter. The angry Javanese monarch fitted out his navy, secretly sailed up the Mekong, and conquered Chenla. He took the life of no one but the foolish prince, whose head he presented to the prince's successor as a warning.

During the troubled period toward the close of the eighth century, the future founder of a new Khmer state, young Jayavarman II, went to Java to live. There he learned the techniques by which the Javanese monarch, a Hindu, had established rule over that country. When Jayavarman II returned to his chaotically splintered homeland, he conquered and pacified it. After establishing a series of capitals on the inland plain, relatively remote from Java, he proclaimed himself a Universal Monarch and ceased to pay tribute to Java.

Jayavarman II initiated a new religious cult based on the Javanese model, calling himself "King of the Mountain," a title that traditionally had been both Javanese and Khmer. He claimed that, through the medium of a Brahman priest, divinity had been bestowed on him by Shiva, the Hindu god of creation and destruction of the universe. The king's spiritual and temporal essence resided in the *lingam,* the phallic form of Shiva. The *lingam* was called the *devarāja,* meaning god-king; the king's living superhuman spirit was as fully present in it as in the god-king himself. The *devarāja* was enshrined in the center of a monumental religious complex, representing the spiritual axis of the kingdom, where, the people believed, their divinely ordained king communicated with the gods.

All parts of Khmer society focused on and worked for the glory of the god-king, just as the pyramid temple, with his royal essence, the *devarāja,* was the architectural center of the kingdom. The Khmer people accepted a life of service to the god-king as the duty imposed on them by birth. They believed the Indian concept that death is followed by rebirth, that one's position in this life is determined by his actions in a previous life.

For instance, if one acted nobly and generously in this life, in the next life he would be reborn a king or a priest. The unrighteous person who did not perform the duties or religious ceremonies prescribed by his station would be reborn a slave or a toad.

Each category in Khmer society performed a specified task; the individual had no choice. The services of the priestly class were essential to the ceremonies of the god-king. The Brahman priests were also the educators; there was no secular education. Learning included knowledge of the scriptures, in order to understand better how to serve the gods and the god-king. Another class consisted of such guilds of artisans as gem-cutters, bronze-casters, wrestlers, who in the service of the god-king exercised the skill designated at birth. The hardest-working group were the peasants;

*The four faces of Lokeshvara on a tower built by Jayavarman VII. Late 12th–early 13th century* A.D. *A European archaeologist watches the natives clear away the jungle roughly six hundred and fifty years later. This drawing appeared in Louis Delaporte's folio* Voyage au Cambodge, *published in 1880 in Paris*

they owned land but had to share their crops with the king and the monasteries. When called upon by the god-king, they were required to build monuments that immortalized him. In times of war the same peasant-builder was also expected to become a soldier for the god-king. He was led into battle by his own village headman, whom the king appointed captain. The captain swore abiding loyalty to the king, and in turn extracted loyalty from the peasant. There also were slaves, both hill tribesmen who had not come under the civilizing Indian influences, and prisoners of war. While they performed the least desirable tasks, they were not the backbone of the labor force; the largest amount of work was carried out by the peasant-builder-soldier.

During the Angkor period the Khmers did not question their religious system. It ordered their lives, regulating everything from agriculture (including water conservation) to birth and death rites. The peasant-builder who toiled at the construction of the king's monuments believed that this work would assure him a favored position in his next life. Like the priest or gem-cutter, he accepted his fate as part of the earthly scheme which, if carried out properly, would ensure prosperity and well-being for all.

Until their fortunes faded in the late thirteenth century, the Khmers had no incentives for radical change. Their architecture reflects the static quality of life during this era; it mirrors their unchanging belief in the god-king who was at the center of their known world. Only minor technological advances occurred, such as a progression in major building materials from brick in the tenth century to sandstone in the eleventh century. The same stories were told and retold in reliefs because the people continued to believe that they represented the truth. The pantheon of gods remained constant, with only minor shifts in the relative importance of individual gods. It is presumed that Chou Ta-kuan's thirteenth-century account of life in Angkor, frequently quoted here, reflects a life style similar to that which prevailed at the court in earlier times.

Following the example of Jayavarman II, succeeding monarchs continued to install themselves as god-king and command the loyalty of the people. Shiva worship was not introduced by Jayavarman II; it had been previously practiced in old Funan, just as previous local kings had been called "King of the Mountain." But Jayavarman II combined Shiva worship with the kingship, assuming the role of a Universal Monarch who governed both spiritual and temporal spheres. He brought from Java the theocratic principle associating Shiva with the king.

As Jayavarman II forged his new state, his successive capitals represented progressive pacification and stability. In each capital he built a sanctum containing the *devarāja,* which became the spiritual and temporal focus of the kingdom. Roluos, on the Angkor plain, which had probably been the site of a previous city, was occupied and rebuilt by Jayavarman II during two periods of his reign. It is not clear, however, which building at that site contained his *devarāja*.

The buildings at Roluos that have been identified were built by Indravarman (reigned 877–889), successor to Jayavarman II's son, and also by Indravarman's son. Indravarman installed himself as god-king and built Bakong at Roluos in 881 to house his *devarāja*. The investiture of power, bestowing the gift of divinity on the king from Shiva, was performed by a Brahman priest; this ceremony became an essential rite of kingship which was practiced continuously into modern times.

Bakong is an early example of a temple on the Angkor plain, built to embody the Indian cosmological ideas adopted by the Khmers, particularly the idea of a mountain as central axis of the earth. It was thought that the goal of harmony between heaven and earth could be attained by re-creating the form of the universe in miniature. Since the Roluos site was flat, Indravarman constructed his own mountain—Bakong —in the form of a step pyramid. The central pyramid is surrounded by four enclosures. The first is a laterite wall at the base of the pyramid; the second, a wide moat surrounded by walls. Outside the moat was another wall, and beyond that the outside enclosure, a moat with an earthen embankment which once had a wall of wooden stakes. The moats served both as protection against invaders and as a symbol of the great waters alongside the rock wall of the earth.

The tower sanctuary on top of the five-tiered Bakong pyramid, which housed the *devarāja,* was originally made of light materials, probably wood. The existing tower, probably erected several centuries after the pyramid was built, is very similar to the towers of Prambanam in Java that were built in the ninth century, also under the influence of Indian culture and architecture.

The tower is cruciform—a cubic cell with four projecting doorways. Three of the doors are false; only the eastern door leads to the cult object. The tower rises above the cell in a pattern of repeating roof lines that diminish in scale to the pinnacle. This tower motif is based on Indian prototypes which have roofs that appear stacked one on top of another. Inside the tower, a corbeled vault that employs overlapping bricks carries the roof weight. Since this relatively primitive vaulting system continued to be used throughout the Angkor period without any major technological advances, the tower sanctums could never be much larger.

Other small towers of similar design were geometrically arranged on the fourth level of the pyramid and around its base. These tower sanctuaries housed images of Hindu gods to whom they were dedicated. Dead members of the royal and priestly families were linked with gods in an

23

eternal union. In this way the divine relationship was extended beyond the king himself and the cult of ancestor worship was perpetuated. Libraries to store the sacred scriptures, whose existence was noted in third-century Chinese records, were also built within the ceremonial center.

Two other monuments at the Roluos site, Preah Ko, built by Indravarman in 879, and Lolei, built by his son Yashovarman in 893, have many characteristics in common. Both were dedicated to the parents and grandparents of the kings who built them. Neither has a pyramid center like Bakong, because pyramid temples were built exclusively by the king for his *devarāja,* whereas he erected single-level shrines to honor his ancestors. Like Bakong and the succeeding Angkor monuments, they were surrounded by a series of four concentric enclosures, and like almost all of those monuments except Angkor Wat, they face east. The six brick towers of Preah Ko are on a low platform. Six similar towers were planned for Lolei but only four were built. Wall motifs, like the *kāla* monster head spewing out an exuberantly entwined leafy garland, can be traced back to the Indian Buddhist stupa decoration of Amarāvatī, built seven hundred years earlier; but they also show a direct borrowing of form from Prambanam and other contemporaneous Javanese monuments.

The basic building materials used at Roluos were brick and soft laterite stone; doorways, niches, and freestanding sculpture were of sandstone, and decoratively molded plaster covered the brick walls. This combination remained standard for the construction of sacred monuments for the next hundred years.

Indravarman extended the empire of Jayavarman II. A laudatory inscription, which may well exaggerate his feats, states: "His rule was like a crown of jasmine on the lofty head of the kings of China, Champa, and Java."[1]

Why Jayavarman II selected the Angkor plain area for his capital, and why his successors chose to remain there, cannot be simply answered. On the one hand, its inland position was less accessible to seafaring invaders than were the coastal areas. Another great natural advantage of the Angkor plain was its easy access to the Great Lake of Tonle Sap. Each spring when the Himalayan snows melted, the swollen waters of the Mekong River descended from Tibet, through China, Laos, Thailand, Cambodia, and Vietnam, with such force that the Mekong reversed the current of the Tonle Sap River, which connects the Great Lake with the Mekong, and flooded the Great Lake from July to January. As the waters receded, the Great Lake became a giant fish trap from which the Khmers could easily harvest great amounts of food.

On the other hand, without water storage the land use was extremely limited. To make the land support the population, the state eventually had to expend a tremendous amount of its labor resources to build and maintain the reservoir system. Indravarman built a large *baray,* or reservoir, at Roluos, which was filled by a combination of ground water and rain water brought by the May-to-October monsoon. This man-made lake not only symbolized the divine waters and served ritual purposes, but was also essential to agriculture. Its stored water irrigated the sandy plain, which was naturally arid for six months, and transformed it into a rich rice bowl through all seasons. Ultimately, the water system became so large and elaborate that in the thirteenth century the state, weakened by a series of wars and by extravagant building projects, could no longer muster from its subjects and slaves the labor force necessary to maintain it. The demands of the water system proved to be a major factor contributing to the downfall of the Khmer state.

Yashovarman (reigned 889–900) was Indravarman's son and successor. In 893 he built Lolei, the first of his many monuments, on an island in the middle of Indravarman's *baray.* After several years at Roluos, he decided to build a new capital roughly twelve miles away on the Angkor plain. He may have moved to what we now know as the city of Angkor because Roluos was too crowded or because he had a far grander vision of a capital than did his predecessor. Perhaps he simply had to build his own new temple because Indravarman's pyramid temple, Bakong, not only housed his father's *devarāja* during his lifetime but also served as his funerary temple and therefore could not be used by another.

At Angkor as well as at Roluos, both the palaces of the king and the ruling classes and the living quarters of the ordinary people have disappeared, because these structures were made of wood or other perishable materials. Only the buildings dedicated to the gods were made of stone, and they alone survive.

At Angkor, Yashovarman selected the natural hill of Phnom Bakheng as the center of his new city and built a temple on top of it to house his *devarāja.* His city was called Yashodharapura—"city endowed with splendor"—a name that was used for Angkor during the succeeding six centuries. To support the multiplying population he also built the Eastern Baray, almost five miles long, far vaster than the *baray* at Roluos. Along the southern bank of the *baray,* inscriptions tell us that a series of monasteries was built, one probably Buddhist and the others dedicated to Hindu sects that worshiped Shiva and Vishnu. Official Shiva worship did not exclude devotion to other gods; other sects were tolerated, or even officially assisted. This attitude of peaceful coexistence between Hindu and

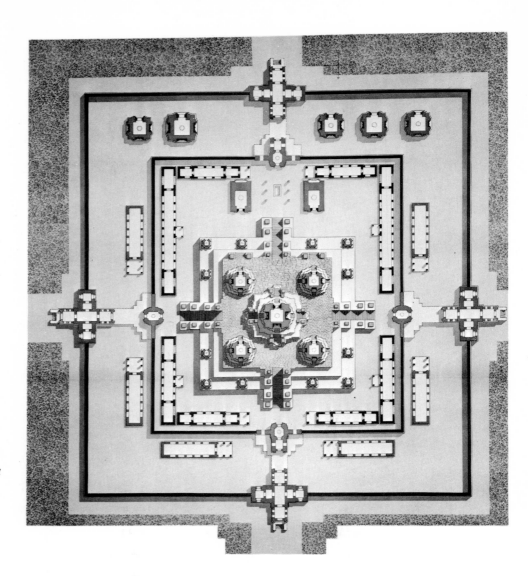

*Plan of Pre Rup. Drawn by Louis Delaporte and published in* Monuments du Cambodge *in 1914*

Buddhist creeds permeated the Indianized civilizations of Southeast Asia.

Succeeding kings continued to build in the great new city of Yashod-harapura until the second quarter of the tenth century, when a series of struggles for power diverted their energies. During the third decade of the tenth century, the victorious king left Angkor with his *devarāja* and built a new capital at Koh Ker, northeast of Angkor. Subsequently a massive ceremonial complex was built at Koh Ker. In 944, Rājendravarman won the throne and returned to the abandoned Angkor site, which he restored. According to an inscription he "made it superb and charming by constructing a palace with a sanctuary of brilliant gold."[2]

Rājendravarman seems to have followed the Roluos models. He built Eastern Mebon on a man-made island in the Eastern Baray and dedicated it to his parents in 952. South of Eastern Mebon and the Baray, he built the great pyramid temple of Pre Rup, principally to house his *devarāja,* but also to honor ancestors in the secondary towers.

An important innovation of Eastern Mebon and Pre Rup is that the sanctuary at the top is no longer a single tower, with smaller outlying towers only on lower tiers of the pyramid. Instead, the central sanctuary itself is composed of five towers—a central one and four others arranged about it so as to form a square, like the five dots on a pair of dice. This

26

five-tower central sanctuary, like the single-tower sanctuary of Bakong, is surrounded by smaller towers on the outer, lower levels. This more complicated plan would reach its final development almost a hundred and fifty years later at Angkor Wat.

The Brahman priests traditionally had had great importance and power as advisors to the king, and their position was enhanced in the *devarāja* ceremony essential to the cult of the god-king. According to one inscription, among the important Brahmans in this period was a prime minister who was called "great advisor to the royal family"[3]; another filled the traditional role of royal chaplain; and a third was the supervisor of the building of sacred monuments. The king granted land to those Brahmans he wished to reward, and some of them were wealthy and powerful enough to build monuments themselves; their temples, like the ancestor temples of Preah Ko and Lolei, were different in form and concept from the mountain-pyramid temples.

Banteay Srei, some fifteen and a half miles north of Angkor, was dedicated in 967 by a Brahman. Surely its *baray* water was used to irrigate the

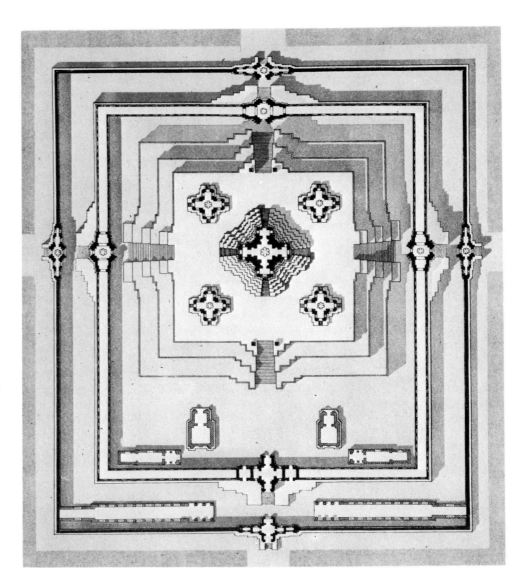

*Plan of Ta Keo. Drawn by Louis Delaporte and published in* Monuments du Cambodge *in 1914*

*Reconstructed elevation of Phimeanakas.*
*Drawn by Louis Delaporte and published in*
Monuments du Cambodge *in 1914*

rice fields in that area, and its sanctuary may have served as the regional religious center. At Banteay Srei's center, a low platform holds three towers, two dedicated to Shiva and one to Vishnu. Their delicate sculptural decoration draws upon the scriptures to tell of the adventures of the gods. The sculptor's hand infused the brilliantly carved pink sandstone with human warmth.

During the next hundred years, three kings built three massive pyramid temples at Angkor: Phimeanakas, Ta Keo, and Baphuon. Although they appear similar to the Bakong prototype at Roluos, they all incorporate innovations in style and construction. Rectangular covered galleries with windows surround the top of Phimeanakas and Baphuon. These top galleries and the lower-level galleries found on Ta Keo and Baphuon were features that, along with the five-tower plan, would reach maturity in the brilliant twelfth-century funerary temple of Angkor Wat.

Ta Keo was the first large pyramid temple to be built completely of sandstone, a harder material than laterite. Its decorative carving was not completed, but why it was left unfinished is a puzzle. Perhaps it was abandoned because the royal patron builder died or was deposed; perhaps the craftsmen found the surface too hard to work and gave up on the relief decorations. Baphuon was mentioned by Chou Ta-kuan, the Chinese envoy who visited Angkor several hundred years later; he reported that its great tower was made of bronze and that it was "truly marvelous" to behold.[4]

# Preah Ko

1. *Preah Ko, Roluos, central towers.* A.D. *879.*
*Brick, laterite, sandstone, and plaster*

Preah Ko was built by Indravarman, who dedicated it to his parents, maternal grandparents, Jayavarman II, founder of the Khmer Empire, and Jayavarman II's wife. The six brick towers rest on a low platform in the center of the ceremonial complex; the front row of towers was devoted to Indravarman's male ancestors and the second row to the female. Inside each tower, the dead ancestor was represented in the image of a Hindu god with whom he or she was assumed to be eternally united.

2. *Preah Ko, Roluos, ceremonial roadway.* A.D. *879.*
*Brick, laterite, sandstone, and plaster*

As one looks back from the central tower platform, a ceremonial roadway runs through a series of ruined gateways in the four sets of concentric rectangular walls that enclose Preah Ko. Royal lions with neatly curled manes guard the stairway to the sanctuary platform. Preah Ko means sacred bull; the stone image that sits on the roadway represents the bull Nandi, the mount of the Hindu god Shiva.

3. *Preah Ko, Roluos, lower section of a tower.* A.D. *879.*
*Brick, laterite, sandstone, and plaster*

The lower portion of each tower consists of a rectangular cell with porches extending in the four directions of the compass. The eastern door leads to the image of the Hindu god linked with the dead ancestor, and the other three doors are false. All the towers were elaborately decorated with carved stone doorways and stone niches in the walls, and the brick walls were covered with a molded plaster design.

4. *Preah Ko, Roluos, detail of tower wall.* A.D. *879.*
*Brick, laterite, sandstone, and plaster*

A series of horizontal moldings embellishes the tower base. Above, a niche contains a divine female figure. She wears a Khmer crown and a full-skirted sarong girdled just below the waist; she was once decoratively swathed in plaster over what is now bare brick.

5. *Preah Ko, Roluos, detail of plaster decoration on tower wall.* A.D. *879. Brick, laterite, sandstone, and plaster*

In this small but revealing remnant one can see the exuberantly molded decoration that once covered all the walls. Above the niche of a god, a *kāla* spews out swirling garlands of foliage beneath his toothy grin. Contemporary Hindu monuments in Java had similar *kāla* faces decorating walls and doorways.

# Bakong

6. *Bakong, Roluos, distant view.* A.D. *881.*
*Brick, laterite, sandstone, and plaster*

Bakong was the large temple pyramid built by Indravarman to contain
his royal essence—the *devarāja*, Shiva's *lingam* or phallus bestowed on the
Khmer kings by Shiva through the medium of a Brahman priest. Bakong
also served as Indravarman's funerary temple.

7. *Bakong, Roluos, gateway entrance to enclosure.* A.D. *881. Brick, laterite, sandstone, and plaster*

Bakong was built in the likeness of Mt. Meru, the residence of the gods at the center of the world. The pyramid temple that suggests the mountain was surrounded by three concentric stone walls, rectangular in shape, and outside, a rectangular earthen embankment. These represented the rock wall of the earth; moats symbolized the great waters. On the north, south, east, and west, passages through the wall shown here (the third one out from the central pyramid) are marked by elaborate gateways guarded by royal lions.

8. *Bakong, Roluos, the pyramid temple.* A.D. *881.*
*Brick, laterite, sandstone, and plaster*

At the center of Bakong is a five-step pyramid, crowned with the tower containing the *devarāja*. The present sandstone tower was erected several hundred years after the pyramid, because the original tower had perished. The tower's cruciform design is formed by four doorways projecting from a square cell. Stairways ascend the four sides of the pyramid; on each level, lions guard both sides of the stairs. Elephants stand at the corners of the five levels on the diagonal axes. The design of the roof is repeated in five superimposed tiers, diminishing in scale to the peak.

9. *Bakong, Roluos, buildings and walkways at the base of the pyramid.* A.D. *881. Brick, laterite, sandstone, and plaster*

Smaller versions of the central tower are repeated at the fourth level of the pyramid and around the base. Within each corbel-vaulted sanctum are images of Hindu deities who were linked with dead ancestors of the king and of Brahman priests who had given spiritual guidance to the kings. Libraries to store the sacred scriptures were also built at the base of the pyramid.

10. *Bakong, Roluos, a god at the base of the pyramid.* A.D. *881.*
*Brick, laterite, sandstone, and plaster*

A headless god stands within the enclosure near Bakong's base. The finely
modeled torso of the god contrasts sharply with his heavy, elephantine
legs. Before the Angkor period, supporting rods held up standing images.
In the Angkor period, the legs of the images were enlarged to assure
stability without supports.

# Lolei

11. *Lolei, Roluos, tower.* A.D. *893. Brick, laterite, sandstone, and plaster*

Yashovarman I constructed Lolei on an island in the middle of the *baray*, or reservoir, built by his father. Its towers were dedicated to the king's parents and grandparents following the Preah Ko model. Originally six brick-and-stone towers were planned, but only four were built.

12.   *Lolei, Roluos, general view.* A.D. *893. Brick, laterite, sandstone, and plaster*

During a thousand years, the brick towers have largely disintegrated. The sandstone doorways and niches have survived better than the brick. Hardly any of the original plaster decoration remains.

# Prasat Kravan

13. *Prasat Kravan, distant view.* A.D. *921. Brick and plaster*

Prasat Kravan was built by high court dignitaries in the same year that a dissident king moved the capital away from Angkor. The monument has an unusual plan, with five brick towers in a row. However, like the ancestor temples of Preah Ko and Lolei, it was built on a single level. Prasat Kravan was dedicated to the Hindu god Vishnu, who appears in a carved bas-relief on the central sanctuary wall.

14. *Prasat Kravan, wall relief, interior of central tower.* A.D. *921. Brick and plaster*

A relief carving shows a feat of Vishnu recounted in the most ancient Indian scriptures: he takes one of the three steps that are all he needs to span the universe. The shining black stone in the foreground is the top of a *lingam*, the phallic symbol of Shiva, placed in the center of the cell sanctum. Although the shrine is dedicated to Vishnu, the presence of Shiva's *lingam* illustrates the syncretic aspect of Khmer Hindu worship.

15. *Prasat Kravan, relief of Lakshmi, interior of a side tower.* A.D. *921. Brick and plaster*

In another tower, Vishnu's voluptuous consort Lakshmi is carved out of the brick wall. Because the roof has disappeared, natural light now bathes Lakshmi, who holds the symbols of her powers in four hands and is flanked by kneeling admirers. The group of three figures resides within a fluidly curving niche which is hung with carved tassels and jewels.

# Baksei Chamkrong

16. *Baksei Chamkrong, general view. First quarter of 10th century.*
*Brick, laterite, sandstone, and plaster*

This delicately proportioned temple pyramid was built at the foot of
Mt. Bakheng by Harshavarman I. He dedicated it to his father, Yashovarman I, who founded the city of Angkor and who had made Mt. Bakheng
the mystical center of his city. An inscription on a column tells that in
947, about twenty-five years after the monument was constructed, a
golden image of Shiva was placed inside the temple.

# Eastern Mebon

17. *Eastern Mebon, view of pyramid corner with an elephant.*
A.D. *952. Brick, laterite, sandstone, and plaster*

Built on a man-made island in the Eastern Baray, Eastern Mebon was
dedicated in 952 to the parents of King Rājendravarman. Its step pyramid
holds five towers representing the five peaks of Meru. Elephants harnessed
with ropes and decorated with bells stand ceremoniously at the corners
of the pyramid levels.

# Pre Rup

18. *Pre Rup, view of pyramid and central towers.* A.D. *961.*
*Brick, laterite, sandstone, and plaster*

Less than a decade after Eastern Mebon was built by Rājendravarman, the same king erected Pre Rup directly south of it on the shore of the Eastern Baray. Following but enlarging the form of Eastern Mebon, the step pyramid of Pre Rup is crowned by five towers.

19. *Pre Rup, tower sanctum.* A.D. 961.
*Brick, laterite, sandstone, and plaster*

The towers on the top tier of the pyramid are arranged one on each corner and one in the center, like five dots on a pair of dice. The central tower housed the king's *lingam* and the other four towers held images honoring the king and his ancestors. The plaster decoration that once covered these towers and the towers on lower levels of the pyramid has disappeared over the centuries.

20. *Pre Rup, view of courtyard and gateways of enclosure walls.* A.D. *961. Brick, laterite, sandstone, and plaster*

Pre Rup had the customary four stairways ascending the pyramid, one in each direction of the compass. At the base, the stairways were met by ceremonial roadways bisecting the concentric rectangular enclosure walls. On each side, access to the complex was possible through three doorways crowned by elaborate gateway towers, which are now in ruins.

# Banteay Srei

21. *Banteay Srei, roadway within the forecourt enclosure.*
A.D. *967. Sandstone and laterite*

A stone roadway, lined with freestanding stone posts, leads to the two central enclosures. Covered terraces, of which only the columns remain, once lined both sides of the roadway.

*22. Banteay Srei, gateway to the second enclosure.*
A.D. *967. Sandstone and laterite*

The gateway leading to the second enclosure has a pediment of most unusual form. The stones faithfully follow the form of diagonal wooden roof beams until they meet in a diamond medallion at the peak, which is fancifully encircled by a flame shape and carved with a design of leaves and gods. The outer ends rise up in a reverse curve coiling like a serpent's tail, crested with a tongue of flame.

23. *Banteay Srei, detail of gateway to the second enclosure.* A.D. 967. *Sandstone and laterite*

Twin pediments crown each end of the roofed gateway. At Banteay Srei, finely carved sandstone decoration replaces the plaster-coated carved brick decoration of earlier monuments. However, there is a continuity of motif; for example, within the triangular frame of the beams is a grinning *kāla* with curling horns of foliage and body tentacles.

24. *Banteay Srei, entrance porch to center of complex.*
A.D. *967. Sandstone and laterite*

Another enclosure wall surrounds the central sanctuary and is marked by a more traditionally styled gateway. The doorway is flanked by a series of piers, one pair carved in the facets of a polygon, the others flat, with delicately carved foliage; over the door the lintel is more deeply incised, with gods and demons in floral garlands. Windows in the enclosure walls have balusters that look like wooden turnings transformed into stone.

25. *Detail of Plate 24*

On top of the gateway, above the door lintel, the edges of the pediment peak and then diverge into sinuous curves descending on each side. Tongues of flame dance along the entire edge. A many-armed god, surrounded by demons holding garlands, dances within the pediment frame to the rhythms of two musicians in the lower corners.

26. *Banteay Srei, lion in front of entrance porch to center of complex.*
A.D. *967. Sandstone and laterite*

A pair of lions guards the entrance porch. The lions' manes, eyebrows, and whiskers appear perfectly curled into neatly organized patterns. Their solid front legs are stiffly planted and seem strangely combined with their raised buttocks and curving back legs, which look ready to spring.

27. *Banteay Srei, detail of a lintel with Indra riding his three-headed elephant.* A.D. 967. *Sandstone and laterite*

Indra, bringer of rains and thunder, king of heaven, and master of the rainbow, which is his bow, is carved on the lintels over the doorways at Banteay Srei and many other Angkor temples. He is shown seated on his three-headed elephant in the middle of the rainbow, which is also the bridge between heaven and earth. His presence symbolizes the worshiper's departure from the world of men into the temple, which is the realm of the gods.

28. *Banteay Srei, central tower with adjoining halls and second tower.* A.D. *967. Sandstone and laterite*

Within the innermost enclosure are the three main towers of Banteay Srei, two of which are dedicated to Shiva and one to Vishnu. Inside the gateway, one passes through two successive halls to the central tower, seen here at the right rear. All three towers share a common platform with the adjoining halls.

29. *Banteay Srei, miniature tower on roof of the main tower.* A.D. *967. Sandstone and laterite*

This miniature tower decorates a corner of the roofline of the larger tower that it reproduces. The scale of Banteay Srei itself is tiny compared to the massive pyramid temples of Angkor; the doorways to the sanctum towers are barely five feet high. Originally dedicated in 967 by an important Brahman priest, Banteay Srei suffered almost a thousand years of disintegration which was accelerated by the work of twentieth-century thieves until the École Française d'Extrême-Orient supervised its reconstruction in the 1920s.

30. *Banteay Srei, east end of north library.*
A.D. *967. Sandstone and laterite*

Two libraries are included within the central enclosure. The rectangular library is divided into three parts: a high central hall with two lower aisles on each side. The façades at both ends, one with a door and the other with a false door, have a progression of three carved pediments, the second and third rising above and behind the first.

31. *Banteay Srei, "The Rain of Indra," detail of east end of north library.* A.D. *967. Sandstone and laterite*

Indra on his three-headed elephant oversees a double rainbow, which takes the form of two *nāga* garlands on the lintel over the doorway. Above the lintel, within the pediment, Indra and his elephant appear again, this time as the source of the gentle life-giving rain. Krishna, one of the incarnations of Vishnu, and his half-brother Balarama are shown on either side at the bottom of the pediment, appreciating the milk of heaven together with men, animals, and plants.

*32. Banteay Srei, detail of pediment, east end of
north library.*

The graceful pediment edges terminate with a lion who emerges from
the mouth of a *makara,* which looks something like a crocodile. The
profile of the *makara* exhibits a bulging eye, bared teeth, and a nose that
extends like an elephant's trunk. The hardness of the pink sandstone
that is employed exclusively on the exterior of the monument allows the
plant, animal, and celestial decor to take on a crisp finish.

33. *Banteay Srei, pediment end.* A.D. *967. Sandstone and laterite*

At the corner of this pediment, a five-headed *nāga* snake issues out of a double-profiled *makara*. The *nāga* is not only the rainbow bridge between heaven and earth, but many other aspects in Khmer and Indian mythology as well—among them, an earth and water spirit, the mythical progenitor of the Khmer people, and the great snake on which Vishnu sleeps at the bottom of the cosmic ocean after the destruction of the universe and before its re-creation.

34. *Banteay Srei, detail of "Battle between Vali and Sugriva," pediment of an annex building in main complex.* A.D. *967. Sandstone and laterite*

Decorating another building at Banteay Srei, a pediment depicts one of the adventures of Vishnu that is recounted in the *Rāmāyana*. Rama (Vishnu in human form) helps the deposed monkey king Sugriva kill his brother Vali, the usurper. In the continuous narrative style, the monkey brothers are shown locked in battle in the center, while on the right Rama shoots a fatal arrow at Vali; on the left, Vali dies.

# Phimeanakas

35. *Phimeanakas, view of enclosure and pyramid. Last quarter of
10th century. Laterite and sandstone*

Phimeanakas may have been built in light materials in the third quarter
of the tenth century by one king and rebuilt in the form of the great stone
pyramid by another king a quarter of a century later. Whereas Mt.
Bakheng had been the first spiritual center of Yashodharapura (Angkor),
Phimeanakas became the new center of the city when Angkor was rebuilt
after being abandoned for twenty years following a series of dynastic
struggles. At this time the monarch built his wooden royal palace within
the Phimeanakas enclosures, as many other kings would do during the
next five centuries.

36. *Phimeanakas, pyramid with gallery around top. Last quarter of 10th century. Sandstone and laterite*

Lions guard each side of all four stairways at the three levels of the step pyramid. A tower covered with gold once stood at the top, but has since perished. Chou Ta-kuan, the Chinese envoy who visited Angkor in the thirteenth century, relates the popular mythology connected with this tower: "The king sleeps in the summit of the palace's golden tower. All the people believe that the tower is also inhabited by the Lord of the Sun who is a nine-headed serpent. Every night the serpent appears in the form of a woman with whom the king sleeps during the first watch. None of the royal wives are allowed in the tower. The king leaves at the second watch to go to his wives and concubines. If the *nāga* spirit does not appear one night, it is a sign that the king's death is imminent. Should the king fail to visit the *nāga* for a single night, the welfare of the kingdom will suffer dire consequences."[5]

*37. Phimeanakas, gallery with windows at top of pyramid. Last quarter of 10th century. Sandstone and laterite*

The most unusual feature of Phimeanakas is the narrow covered gallery around the top. This may have been added by Sūryavarman I, a usurper who gained power early in the eleventh century. The gallery wall is punctuated with windows, and the stone roof has ribs that may originally have held tiles.

# Ta Keo

38. *Ta Keo, distant view. First quarter of 11th century. Sandstone*

It is possible that Ta Keo was begun at the end of the tenth century by the builder of Phimeanakas and finished by Sūryavarman I. It is situated just south of the Avenue of Victory that leads from Phimeanakas to the Eastern Baray. The first Angkor monument to be constructed entirely of sandstone, this pyramid temple has five towers on top. The central one housed the king's *devarāja* and later served as his funerary temple.

*39. Ta Keo, view of enclosure and pyramid temple. First quarter of 11th century. Sandstone*

The central tower is elevated about eighteen and a half feet above the surrounding four towers; the entire pyramid has a total height of nearly 230 feet. Previous tower sanctuaries had entrances only on the east side; these have open access on four sides. A covered gallery with windows, slightly wider than the one at the top of Phimeanakas, runs around the pyramid just above the base.

40. *Ta Keo, detail of pyramid. First quarter of 11th century.*
*Sandstone*

Decoration of the sandstone monument was never completed, possibly because the craftsmen, unaccustomed to such hard surfaces, found them difficult to carve, particularly on so vast a scale. Banteay Srei is covered with intricate carving in sandstone, but it is tiny in comparison.

# Baphuon

41.  *Baphuon, causeway supported by columns. End of 12th century (temple c. 1050–66). Sandstone*

The raised roadway leading to Baphuon was probably built more than a hundred years after the eleventh-century pyramid temple was constructed. It is thought that a great flood engulfed Angkor toward the end of the twelfth century, causing the king to raise the foundations of many structures and to build elevated roadways. This passage linked the pyramid stairs, the libraries within the eastern end of the third enclosure wall, and the eastern gateway of the third enclosure wall.

42. *Baphuon, detail of stacked moldings on pyramid.*
*c. 1050–66. Sandstone*

When Baphuon was built, it became the third center of Yashodharapura
(Angkor), after Mt. Bakheng and Phimeanakas. It was decorated with fine
carvings and bas-reliefs and had a shining copper-colored tower mentioned
by Chou Ta-kuan. This tower, built of perishable materials, has disappeared. Only remnants that suggest its original grandeur can be seen,
such as the stacked moldings beside the pyramid stairs.

43. *Baphuon, a pediment pieced together during reconstruction and held up by wooden supports. c. 1050–66. Sandstone*

When the pyramid of Baphuon was found, the stone parts were quite complete; yet because of faulty construction, half the pyramid had collapsed by the twentieth century. The monument was in the process of being rebuilt in 1970 when the war in Cambodia intervened. Reconstruction is like a giant puzzle, painstakingly fitting all the pieces of each part together as seen here.

# PART II
# ANGKOR WAT

## The Glory of the
## Twelfth Century

# The Glory of the Twelfth Century

Sūryavarman II, twelfth-century builder of Angkor Wat, was one of the kings whose claim to rule rested more on his army than on his inheritance. In 1113 he won the throne in a stunning one-day battle described in an inscription: "Releasing the ocean of his armies on the field of combat, he gave terrible battle; leaping on the head of the elephant of the enemy king, he slew him, just as *garuda* swooping down from the top of a mountain kills a serpent."[6] (*Garuda* was the mythical bird on which the great Hindu deity Vishnu rode.)

The king was an ambitious military leader but it is hard to measure the breadth of his successes. In Thai chronicles and Cham and Northern Vietnamese inscriptions, his enemies recorded forty years of continuous incursion, almost always ending in Khmer defeat. However, another version of these wars is revealed in the history of the Chinese Sung dynasty. Sūryavarman II had sent emissaries to China in 1116 and 1120 to re-establish relations. The Sung history records that Cambodian borders extended to the South China Sea in the east; in the south the country bordered on Champa, the southern part of Vietnam, and the Bay of Bandon in Malaya; and in the west it reached the kingdom of Pagan, centered on the Irrawaddy River in present-day Burma. This vast territorial expanse hardly reflects Khmer defeats.

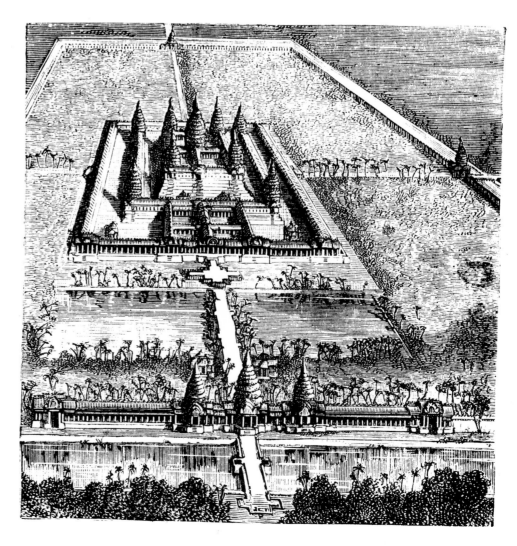

*Bird's-eye view of Angkor Wat. Drawn by Louis Delaporte and published in* Voyage au Cambodge, *1880*

His energy extended beyond his military exploits to include an impressive building program. Thommanon, Chau Say Tevoda, and Angkor Wat are three of the monuments he built. The first two were small shrines built on either side of the Avenue of Victory, the great axial roadway between Phimeanakas and the Eastern Baray. Because Chau Say Tevoda has not been completely cleared of jungle growth, it retains an aspect of Angkor recorded by the French writer Pierre Loti in the nineteenth century: "The fig tree is the ruler of Angkor today. . . . Over the temples which it has patiently pried apart, everywhere its dome of foliage triumphantly unfolds its sleek pale branches speckled like a serpent's skin."[7] *Tevodas*—celestial females—decorate the walls of Chau Say Tevoda, which was intended as a re-creation of a heavenly palace.

The walls surrounding Thommanon have completely disappeared, leaving only the entrance gateways on the east and west ends. Thommanon's tower is joined to an entrance chamber by a small passage; the lower roof of the passage fits into the rhythm of the tower's ascending porch pediments. This use of repeating pediments above the doorways would be more fully elaborated at Angkor Wat.

Because of the quality of carving in the sandstone, the tower profile has great sharpness and compact energy. Although there is a progressively elaborate articulation of elements, the same basic cruciform arrangement seen in earlier monuments persists: a cubic cell sanctum with four projecting porch doorways. The roof line motif occurs five times, each level diminishing in size, until it is crowned by a two-story, full-blown lotus. The porch pediments are repeated twice in each direction; each second pediment is set above and behind the first. The pediment edges meet in a peak and then diverge in a succession of sinuous curves. Open-mouthed *makaras* curve out at the bottom of the pediment edges, spewing forth five-headed *nāgas*. Within this undulating frame appear the stories of Vishnu's ceaseless struggles against the demonic forces of the universe. (According to Indian scriptures, every time the earth is re-created Vishnu appears in ten different avatars, or forms, to kill the oppressive tyrant demons of the earth.)

In the twelfth century a great wave of enthusiastic Vishnu worship swept through India and Southeast Asia, encouraging a more personal devotional relationship to the god than was practiced by the Shivite cults. Because Sūryavarman II devoted himself to Vishnu, the exploits of that god, carved in stone, decorate all the king's structures.

To contain his royal essence, the *devarāja,* and to serve as his funeral monument, Sūryavarman II built the great temple-mountain of Angkor Wat south of the crowded city of Yashodharapura. Like earlier pyramid temples, though on a far grander scale, Angkor Wat is a Khmer repro-

*Ascending passageways within Angkor Wat. Print by H. Clerget after a photograph by M. Gsell published in François Garnier's* Voyage d'Exploration en Indo-Chine *in 1873*

duction of the cosmic order. Its five central towers represent the five peaks of Mt. Meru surrounded by the rock wall of the earth; its vast moat and basins represent the great waters. It, too, has four enclosures: a moat and outer wall, and inside, three rectangular galleries set one within the other. It is a mammoth complex, covering almost a square mile. The architectural harmony of Angkor Wat is outstanding in two respects: in the fluent and lucid integration of the diverse building parts, and in the fusion of the supremely well-carved decoration and the architectural form.

A moat of almost two and a half miles surrounds the outer wall, which has four large ceremonial tower gateways that offer access from the four points of the compass. Within that wall, rectangular reservoirs lie on either side of the western roadway leading to the main portion of the temple. The causeway is lined with great stone balustrades. At intervals, where the causeway juts out at right angles to the direction of the road, the ends of the stone rails curl up into seven-headed *nāgas*. The sacred *nāga* snake has many aspects in Khmer and Indian mythology, as discussed above (see text accompanying Plate 33). Here the *nāga* balustrade represents the rainbow bridge, the link between heaven and earth.

A cruciform platform guarded by stone lions lies on the roadway just in front of the three principal enclosures. Although the precise function of this platform has not been discovered, the king and his court may well have held audiences there. Beyond the platform is the outer gallery, with a triple gateway. Inside, one proceeds through a courtyard with covered halls to the second gallery. Here the devotee crossed another courtyard to climb the steep steps of the sacred mountain, the five-tower central complex. The four corner towers are joined by a rectangular inner gallery, within which two additional halls form a cross at the large central tower, where the *devarāja* is kept in the innermost sanctum. (For a clearer idea of the plan of this great complex, see the bird's-eye view of Angkor Wat drawn by Louis Delaporte, page 93.) The tower profiles follow the

*Angkor Wat, imaginary reconstruction drawn by Louis Delaporte and published in* Voyage au Cambodge *in 1880*

Thommanon model, as do many of the other details. Yet here the multiplication of elements on such a massive scale—the sheer numbers of walls and doorways, with rising pediments and coordinating galleries, terraces, and towers—is so great that it seems superhuman.

A problem for many visitors unfamiliar with Hindu temple architecture is the lack of some large focal hall, such as one is accustomed to find in a church or other kind of temple. These Khmer monuments, following the Indian model, never provided for mass worship of the cult image. The small sanctum cell in the central tower was intended solely to contain the sacred image; it had enough room for only a few privileged people like the king and his priests.

It seems as if no part of Angkor Wat is without decoration. The leaf designs, descended from the vigorously plastered brick of the Roluos group and the sinuous crystalline forms of Banteay Srei, are more restrained, in a shallower relief, more naturally harmonious with the wall itself. There is a new unity of design and wall, as well as a superb fluidity in the carving. *Nāgas, garudas, makaras,* and other mythical beasts guard the roof lines, and the pediments continue to tell of Vishnu's epic adventures.

The celestial females, whose supple charms warm the stone walls, reflect the facial features and the modish styles of the Khmer court. Chou Ta-kuan noted that all beautiful daughters were given to the king to join his retinue of several thousand wives, concubines, and palace attendants, whom Chou described as having skin as white as jade. The envoy, who was himself obviously fascinated by the women, went on to tell how the Chinese spent their days of leisure at the river watching the women bathe. "Arriving at the river bank, the women shamelessly take off their clothes and go into the water joining thousands of other bathers. Even the women of the noble families participate without stigma."[8]

One of the most remarkable series of carvings appears on the walls of the outer galleries, the circumference of which measure more than a half mile. The long wall spaces, too extensive to be taken in at a single glance, are especially well suited to the continuous narrative bas-reliefs. They tell the stories of Vishnu, including the churning of the ocean where Vishnu appears as a tortoise, and the great battles from the Indian epics, the *Rāmāyana* and the *Mahābhārata,* where Vishnu appears as Rama and Krishna. The Khmer troops in all their glory, waging the military campaigns of Sūryavarman II, are depicted as the ground forces of the mythic battles. Sūryavarman II is represented in a refreshingly Khmer variation on this theme; he, along with Rama, Krishna, and others, is shown as an avatar of Vishnu. Indeed, Sūryavarman II not only worshiped Vishnu but also associated his own semidivine person with him. Probably Sūryavarman and his cult worshipers considered the king to be an avatar or earthly form of Vishnu.

Pious artisans and peasants were probably allowed to enter Angkor Wat only as far as the outer gallery. There they would walk around looking at the reliefs and paying homage to the god-king.

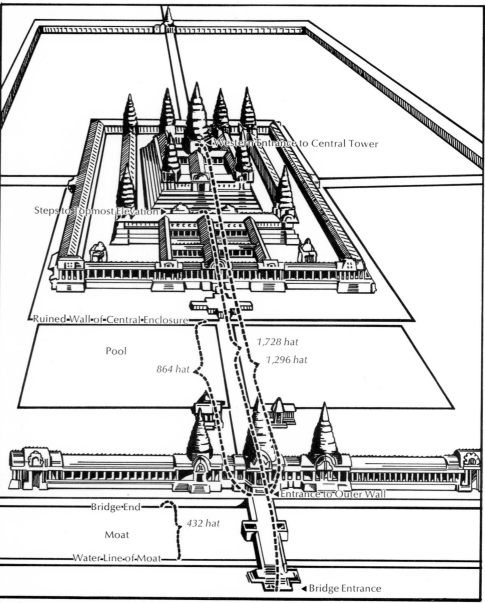

*Bird's-eye view of Angkor Wat, redrawn from Louis Delaporte's drawing, with* yuga *measurements added*

The Khmer unit of measure is the *hat:* 1 *hat* equals about ½ yard

An important new interpretation of Angkor Wat's overall scheme has recently been proposed by Eleanor Morón. She suggests that all the key measurements of the monument, such as the distance from the entrance bridge to the center of the sanctuary, are based on the Khmer concept of time and cosmology, which was adapted from the Indian. According to Indian belief, the duration of the earth is 4,320,000,000 years, which is one thousand *mahayugas*—a single day of Brahma. After this, the earth is burned up and dissolved into the cosmic ocean for an equivalent amount of time—the night of Brahma. Then the process of creation, maintenance, and destruction is repeated, as it has been repeated an infinite number of times.

Each *mahayuga,* 4,320,000 years, is divided into four periods. The first is the *krita yuga,* which consumes 1,728,000 years (four-tenths of a *mahayuga*). This is the golden age, when man is full of goodness. The distance between the entrance to the outer wall and the center of the complex, which is the western stairway to the topmost point of the central enclosure, is 1,728 *hat,* (a *hat* is about half a yard). The second period is the *treta yuga,* of 1,296,000 years (three-tenths of a *mahayuga*), when man is somewhat corrupted by evil. The distance between the entrance to the tower wall and the western entrance to the central tower is 1,296 *hat.* The third *yuga* is the *dvapara yuga,* of 864,000 years (two-tenths of a *mahayuga*), when man is half dominated by greed and corruption. The distance from the entrance gate of the outer wall to the now-ruined wall which once surrounded the three central enclosures and the sanctum is 864 *hat.* The final period, in which we find ourselves today, is the *kali yuga,* of 432,000 years (one-tenth of a *mahayuga*), when man is almost totally without goodness. The distance across the water of the moat is 432 *hat.*

Beyond this, Mrs. Morón has computed the measurements of many parts of the monuments, such as interior spaces and towers, as well as the number of towers and stairs. All of these seem to coincide with the solar or lunar cycles, the number of divinities on Mt. Meru, or one of a host of other cosmologic numerations.

Mrs. Morón's analysis makes it possible to explain the structuring of the Angkor Wat complex in specific cosmologic terms, and invites the possibility of similar interpretations for other Khmer monuments.

# Thommanon

This small complex north of the Avenue of Victory was restored in 1960. The walls surrounding Thommanon have disappeared, leaving only the entrance gateways on the east and west ends. The central tower and its adjoining hall are built on a low platform; a single library to the southeast is the only other building in the complex.

45. *Thommanon, tower and hall. Second quarter of 12th century. Sandstone*

The silhouette of the tower at Thommanon strikes a better balance between material and form than the brick towers of Preah Ko. This tower represents a step in the evolution of style that took place within the confines of an unchanging overall architectural scheme. Whereas earlier buildings were adaptations of wooden buildings (and even here the barrel roof of the entrance chamber, standard for Angkor monuments, looks like an adaptation of a thatched roof in stone), at Thommanon one begins to see the qualities of sandstone exploited. The diminishing circular tower rises with dignity peculiar to stone above the cruciform sanctum with its porches.

46. *Thommanon, gateway pediment with Vishnu on garuda.*
*Second quarter of 12th century. Sandstone*

Over the doorways are twin pediments, the second set above and behind
the first. The pediments, like those of Banteay Srei, have edges that meet
in a peak and then diverge into sinuous curves. Within this undulating
frame, a *garuda* carries the now headless Vishnu into battle against the
demonic forces of the world.

# Chau Say Tevoda

47. *Chau Say Tevoda, distant view. Second quarter of 12th century. Sandstone*

Chau Say Tevoda, just south of Thommanon, is dwarfed by the great temple mountain of Ta Keo to the east, which was built approximately three-quarters of a century earlier. Its plan is similar to that of Thommanon, with a hall linked to the central tower, to libraries, and to enclosing walls with elaborate gateways. The nonexclusive nature of Shiva and Vishnu worship is exemplified by the fact that although the temple was dedicated to Shiva, nearly all the relief carvings show scenes of Vishnu.

48. *Chau Say Tevoda, porchway of the central tower.*
*Second quarter of 12th century. Sandstone*

A mammoth tree has almost consumed the central tower porch on one
side. The walls of all the porchways are decorated with *tevodas,* the celestial females who inhabit the palaces of the gods. While sandstone niches
adorn the tenth-century brick towers at Roluos, here sandstone is used as
the building material throughout, resulting in a more harmonious fusion
of the architectural decoration with the whole.

49. *Chau Say Tevoda, elevated walkway near sanctum. End of 12th century (temple, second quarter of 12th century). Sandstone*

A walkway raised on pillars was added to the temple complex twenty-five to fifty years after it was built. The elevated passage joins the central tower and hall to the libraries and the eastern gateway of the complex. Lichen and mold produced in the jungle moisture have transformed the stone into a mottled kaleidoscope of botanical hues.

# Angkor Wat

50. *Angkor Wat, distant view of outer wall and central towers.*
*Second quarter of 12th century. Sandstone and laterite*

The vast flat plain of Angkor, spotted with trees, is dry for six months
of the year. During this dry season, when the sandy soil can support little
jungle undergrowth, the plain provides an austere setting for the dramatic
temple-mountain of Angkor Wat. A great moat and outer wall define the
extent of this mammoth complex, one of the largest religious creations
in the world. The sacred waters which surround the temple-mountain
were functional as well as symbolic, assuring the success of the life-giving
cycle.

51. *Angkor Wat, western causeway. Second quarter of the 12th century. Sandstone and laterite*

From the main western entrance, a great roadway extends almost a quarter of a mile east to the main part of the complex. The stone causeway is approximately thirty feet wide and is elevated about five feet above ground. Large stone balustrades line the sides of the roadway.

52. *Angkor Wat, outer gallery and central towers reflected in a basin. Second quarter of 12th century. Sandstone*

There are two rectangular basins on either side of the great roadway. In this photograph, the waters of one basin reflect the towers and the outer gallery. Beyond the basins, a low stone wall holds an earth terrace about six feet above the entry level of the outer wall.

53. *Angkor Wat, back of nāga balustrade end along western causeway.*
*Second quarter of 12th century. Sandstone (reconstructed)*

The *nāga*-headed balustrades that line the great western roadway repeat
the *nāga* rainbow-bridge theme seen in the relief sculpture of Banteay
Srei. At intervals sections of the great roadway jut out at right angles. At
the beginning and end of the balustrades, and at these interval points, the
rail ends curl up into giant *nāga* heads. However aesthetically successful
the carved stone form is—a reverse curve fanning out into multiple heads
—these *nāga* heads were unsupported except where they joined the rail,
and were therefore especially vulnerable to accidental damage. They
were also easily dislodged by treasure seekers. This *nāga* head is a modern
reconstruction made under the supervision of the École Française d'Extrême-Orient.

54. *Angkor Wat, front of nāga balustrade end. Second quarter of 12th century. Sandstone (reconstructed)*

The fluid *nāga* railings help to integrate the diverse parts of the monument by accenting the causeway. This artistic reason, plus their symbolic value as a link between the world of men and the world of the gods, doubtless accounts for the fact that the *nāga* balustrade is used throughout the monuments of the twelfth and thirteenth centuries.

*55. Angkor Wat, cruciform platform in front of the outer gallery.
Second quarter of 12th century. Sandstone*

At the end of the great western roadway, a cruciform platform lies in front of the principal part of the complex. Although the precise function of the platform has not been determined, the king and his court may well have used it for holding audiences. Stone lions guard the stairs.

56. *Angkor Wat, section of covered hallway inside the outer gallery. Second quarter of 12th century. Sandstone*

The outer gallery, which is roofed and has small corner towers, includes courtyards and more covered hallways leading to the second gallery and the central tower complex. Throughout Angkor Wat, gallery walls have carved decoration or baluster windows on one side and columned porticoes on the other. The square columns of the portico have simple floral bands on the capitals and bases.

57. *Angkor Wat, detail of doorway within the outer gallery.*
*Second quarter of 12th century. Sandstone*

Many doorways are decorated with the serpentine leafy garlands seen on
earlier temples. Little *devas*—godlings—surrounded by haloes of flame
appear above lotus flowers at intervals down the center of the jamb. A
lotus rosette below each god appears to be the source of the curling
tendrils of the garlands; the vertical edges of the panel are lined with a
row of lotus rosettes.

58. *Angkor Wat, tevoda on wall within the outer gallery. Second quarter of 12th century. Sandstone*

*Tevodas,* the celestial females who inhabit the palaces of heaven, appropriately appear on the walls of this temple—an earthly evocation of the palace of the gods. The facial features of the *tevodas* are modeled after the countless beauties who surrounded the king, and their adornments follow twelfth-century court fashions.

59. *Angkor Wat, tevoda within the outer gallery. Second quarter of 12th century. Sandstone*

This heavenly beauty holding a lotus in each hand stands in a shallow niche, while behind her a second *tevoda* can be seen in another wall niche. Her head is crowned with a three-pronged diadem hung with jewels; a finely woven jeweled collar encircles her neck. Two triple strings of jewels curve in between her full bare breasts and back around her tiny waist; her hips are covered with an intricate girdle hung with more jewels.

60. *Angkor Wat, two tevodas within the outer gallery. Second quarter of 12th century. Sandstone*

Two *tevodas* stand against the wall in completely frontal position except for their feet, which are shown in profile. One wears a single knotted crown and the other a double knotted one over a hair style which fans out on both sides. They wear the Khmer court fashions, with jewels encircling the neck and ankles and a long skirt hung from a jeweled hip girdle. Their skirts have panels shaped like fish tails billowing out to the sides.

61. *Angkor Wat, three tevodas within the outer gallery. Second quarter of 12th century. Sandstone*

Three beauties with interlocked arms decorate this wall corner. Three-pronged diadems with lotuses crown their heads, and their lithe torsos are draped with a finely patterned material. The *tevoda* faces have Khmer features—broad brows and high flat cheekbones, a nose that widens markedly at the bottom, and full lips.

*62. Angkor Wat, steps of the central tower complex. Second quarter of 12th century. Sandstone*

Two galleries surround the heart of the monument, which is the great pyramid base holding the five central towers connected by galleries. The steep climb to the central towers suggests on a small scale the awesome height of the sacred Mt. Meru. Only the inner circle, the king and his priests, would climb these narrow sandstone stairs to the inner sanctum.

63. *Angkor Wat, view from the center to the main entrance. Second quarter of 12th century. Sandstone*

Looking down and back toward the west, one can see the courtyard and second gallery. In the distance the great causeway, two libraries, and the outer walls come into view. Near the center, the roofs of the second gallery rise in steps, reaching maximum height over the center gateway.

64. *Angkor Wat, windows with balusters within the outer gallery. Second quarter of 12th century. Sandstone*

Rows of windows have screens of turned balusters, a motif frequently seen in walls throughout the Angkor monuments. The baluster form is an obvious translation of wooden turnings into stone. No doubt the wooden palaces and fine houses of Angkor were screened in a similar manner.

65. *Angkor Wat, four tevodas within the outer gallery. Second quarter of 12th century. Sandstone*

Four gesturing *tevodas* in a row are a veritable fashion display of various crowns and coiffures. The high polish on their faces and breasts is the result of countless caresses by admiring visitors. Rubbings to reproduce these reliefs are often made by molding wet paper to the contours of the stone and then rubbing a charcoal stick over the paper to record the lines of the sculptured image.

66. *Angkor Wat, a corner tower of the outer gallery.*
*Second quarter of 12th century. Sandstone*

The gallery roofs meet at the corner with a remarkable harmony and artistry. The pattern of ascending roof lines is marked by the elaborately curved pediments seen on so many Angkor monuments. The square corners of the tower base repeat themselves like a many-pointed star, linking the lower square to the circular tower roof.

67. *Angkor Wat, detail of ascending porch roofs at the corner of the outer gallery. Second quarter of 12th century. Sandstone*

In a closer view of the corner tower, the details embellishing the roof lines become apparent. The stories of the gods are carved in the roughly triangular pediments that mark the ends of roof lines. Open-mouthed *makaras* curl up at the pediment ends into diverse mythical beasts—*nāgas, garudas, kālas.*

68. *Angkor Wat, a pediment depicting a scene from the Rāmāyana, within the outer gallery. Second quarter of 12th century. Sandstone*

Most of the pediments over the doorways and at the roof-ends tell the stories of Vishnu. This one shows Vishnu in the guise of Rama with the bow on the right, fighting the ten-headed, twenty-armed demon Ravana on a chariot on the left. The climax of the *Rāmāyana* is this battle scene, when Rama slays the lustful and corrupt Ravana, who had abducted Rama's wife Sita.

69. *Angkor Wat, view from a window of the inner gallery to the second gallery. Second quarter of 12th century. Sandstone*

The gallery wall around the central pyramid, like the others, has windows with baluster screens. We look back over the courtyard in front of the second gallery gateway; the top of the outer gallery is also in view, close behind the second. Beyond it one can see a quadrant of Angkor Wat covered with palms and other tropical trees.

70. *Angkor Wat, bas-relief of a scene from the Mahābhārata, from southern section of the west wall, outer gallery. Second quarter of 12th century. Sandstone*

The long outer gallery walls are covered with narrative bas-reliefs concerning Vishnu. This is a detail of two warriors within the great battle scene where Vishnu, here incarnated as Krishna, aids the five Pandu brothers in their fight against the cousins who cheated them out of the inheritance of their kingdom. Khmer soldiers are shown as the combatants, and the whole scene suggests the martial strength of the twelfth-century imperial forces.

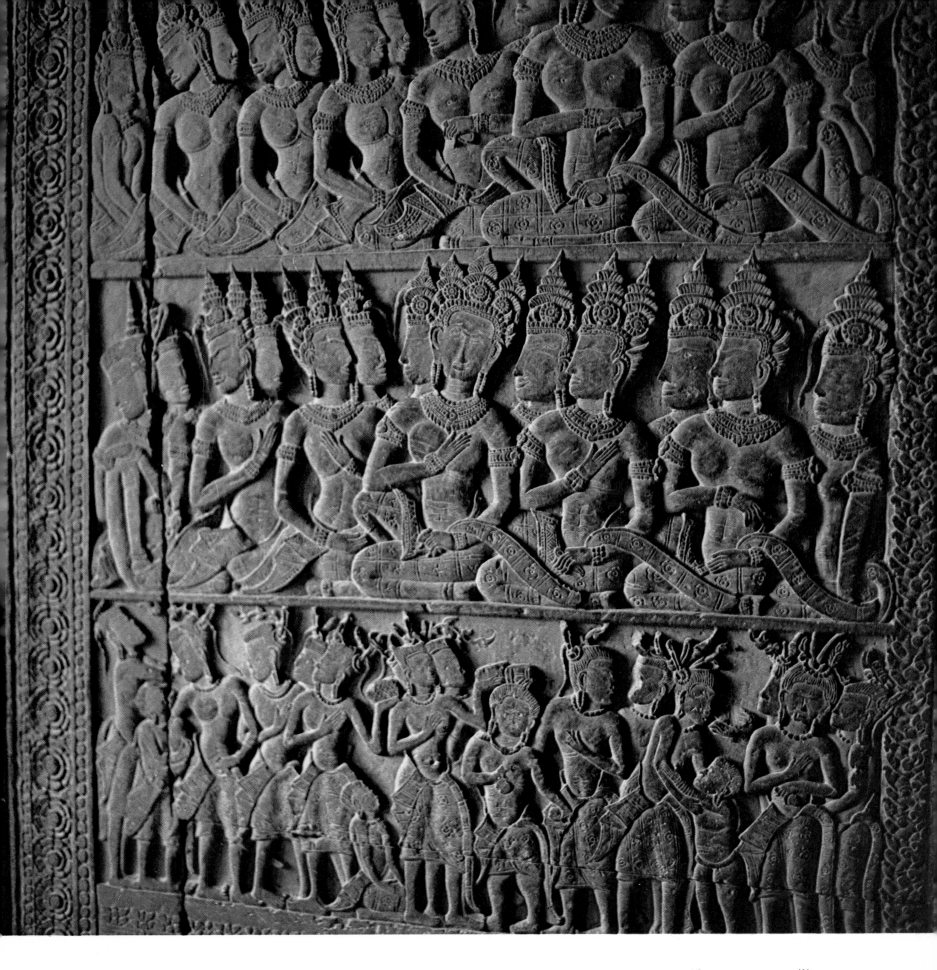

71. *Angkor Wat, bas-relief from the southwest corner tower of the outer gallery. Second quarter of the 12th century. Sandstone*

In the corners of the outer gallery there are cruciform tower pavilions with smaller groups of carvings depicting stories of the gods. These ladies sitting in a row attend a dramatic episode taking place above them. There Shiva burns up Kama, the god of love, because Kama had shot Shiva with one of his arrows at the behest of Parvati, Shiva's ultimate paramour.

72. *Angkor Wat, bas-relief of Sūryavarman II in state, from the western section of the south wall, outer gallery. Second quarter of 12th century. Sandstone*

In a refreshing Khmer variation on the classical avatars of Vishnu, Sūrya-varman II, along with Krishna, Rama, and the others, is shown as a form of Vishnu. The god-king sits in state on a dais with curving *nāga*-legs and a *nāga*-headed balustrade, while his attendants hold umbrellas, fly whisks, and fans.

73. *Angkor Wat, bas-relief of heavens and hells from the eastern section of the south wall, outer gallery. Second quarter of 12th century. Sandstone*

In the middle row, two dignified equestrians lead the blessed to paradise. Above, there is another happy procession which leads to the loftiest regions of the heavens. The lowest register of this relief, shown in Plate 74, shows scenes of hell. Traces of the paint and gilt that once covered the relief can still be seen.

74. *Angkor Wat, bas-relief from the eastern section of the south wall, outer gallery. Second quarter of 12th century. Sandstone*

The individual character of many divisions of heaven and hell seems Dante-like but of course is drawn from the Indian sacred scriptures. The god of death presides over the hells, where the unfortunate damned are punished for the crimes they committed during their lifetimes. Brawny servants of the king of hell bludgeon the emaciated inhabitants of that region while an elephant looks on.

75. *Angkor Wat, bas-relief of a scene from the Rāmāyana, from the northwest corner tower of the outer gallery. Second quarter of 12th century. Sandstone*

After his victory against Ravana, Rama is carried on a palanquin while his monkey allies celebrate the victory joyously. Some dance and clap while others beat the drums and play fish-shaped flutes.

76. *Angkor Wat, bas-relief of a scene from the Rāmāyana, from the northern section of the west wall, outer gallery. Second quarter of 12th century. Sandstone*

In the climax of the *Rāmāyana*, Ravana sits on his battle chariot pulled by a strange beast. Ravana is falsely confident that he can win; he had earned a divine boon which guaranteed that he should not be slain by a god. In the end, Vishnu in the human form of Rama triumphs. Rama's allies surround the oppressive demon, who not only kidnapped Rama's wife but ruled his kingdom with unrighteous and licentious principles abhorrent to good men and to the gods.

77. *Angkor Wat, a group of Buddhas. 12th century and later. Sandstone*

Roughly two or three centuries after Sūryavarman II's reign, when Hīnayāna Buddhism spread over Cambodia, Angkor Wat was turned into a monastery. Buddhist monks placed inside the monument gold-covered images of the Buddha, which they worshiped then and continue to worship today. All parts of the Buddha are sacred, even the footprints that he made while walking and preaching. In the left background a golden image of the Buddha's foot can be seen.

78. *Angkor Wat, Buddha sheltered by Muscalinda. Style of first half of 12th century. Sandstone*

Several versions of the Buddhist scriptures tell the story of a terrible storm that crashed down from heaven when the Buddha was in a trance. Seeing the Buddha unprotected, the *nāga* king Muscalinda lifted up his great head like an umbrella to shield him from the elements. Because of the special significance of the *nāga,* this particular image of the Buddha became a standard representation in Cambodia. He wears an Angkor-style crown with a conical top and jewelry.

79. *Angkor Wat, great western roadway. Second quarter of 12th century. Sandstone*

Nineteenth-century explorers found Angkor Wat in much better condition than most of the other Khmer monuments. Surely its good condition is due to the fact that until the twentieth century, it was continuously inhabited by Buddhist monks who kept back the encroaching jungle growth. The original western roadway within the outer wall can be seen on the right; the left section was rebuilt recently.

# Banteay Samre

80. *Banteay Samre, laterite wall enclosing central complex. Third quarter of 12th century. Laterite and sandstone*

Banteay Samre was built in the troubled period after Sūryavarman II died and before Jayavarman VII, who would build Angkor Thom, ascended the throne. It is not clear who built it and whether it was dedicated to Vishnu or Buddha. It lies about 820 feet east of the southeast end of the Eastern Baray.

81. *Banteay Samre, gateway in laterite wall. Third quarter of 12th century. Laterite and sandstone*

Banteay Samre is small, with decoration of fine quality. Found relatively complete, it was reconstructed by a team from the École Française d'Extrême-Orient. The roof finials seen here, but on no other Angkor monument today, were probably a common feature of many buildings during the Angkor period. If the barrel roof is indeed a translation of a thatched roof into stone, the finials, so decorative here, are adaptations of wooden blocks that functioned as wind baffles to hold down the thatch.

82. *Banteay Samre, central enclosure. Third quarter of 12th century. Laterite and sandstone*

A platform walkway lined by a *nāga* balustrade on the inside of the enclosure wall surrounds the central tower-hall group and two libraries. Two of the four finely finished sandstone gateways of the inner enclosure are in view at the right and in the rear center, contrasting with the rough laterite wall that they cut. The tower-hall can be seen to the left on a high base.

83. *Banteay Samre, a scene from the Rāmāyana, pediment over entrance gateway. Third quarter of 12th century. Sandstone*

As in earlier temples, carved lintels and pediments over the doorways are decorated with floral and mythical motifs relating to Vishnu. Here Vishnu is shown at the left as Rama with a bow, fighting the ten-headed Ravana at the right. Ravana appears again in the center, below a god whose crown is held by celestial spirits.

# PART III
# ANGKOR THOM

## The Final Flowering
## of the Khmer Empire

# The Final Flowering of the Khmer Empire

Jayavarman VII was the last of the great empire and temple builders of the Angkor period. He was born between 1125 and 1130 and his father, Dharanindravarman II, a Buddhist, reigned about 1160. At his father's death, the throne was won not by Jayavarman, but by a claimant whose heritage was legitimate through another branch of the family. Prevented from ruling, Jayavarman VII went into a self-imposed exile. An inscription tells us that in 1166 a usurper overthrew the king, leading Jayavarman's disconsolate wife to urge him to return "to rescue the land from the ocean of misfortune in which it has been plunged."[9] But he was to wait fifteen years to claim the throne and "rescue the land which was weighed down with crimes."[10]

His opportunity came when the ruler of the Chams, eastern neighbors and traditional enemies of the Khmers, initiated a campaign of aggression. Executing a boldly conceived plan, in 1177 the Chams launched a surprise attack after sailing up the Mekong into the Great Lake. Following their victory the usurper king was killed, the city of Angkor sacked and looted, and all portable precious objects carried off by the victors. Jayavarman VII, who was then almost fifty years of age, finally saw his chance to claim the throne, provided he could first rid the land of the Chams. Over a period of four years, in a series of water and land battles, Jayavarman VII was ultimately successful. His investiture in 1181 and his rebuilding of Angkor were described in an inscription: "The city of Yashodharapura, like a young maiden of good family well matched with her fiancé and burning with desire, decorated with a palace of precious stones and clothed in its ramparts, was married by the king for procreation of good fortune for his people [and this was] celebrated by a magnificent feast."[11]

The mature monarch not only vowed revenge against the Chams but also embarked on the most ambitious construction program of any Khmer king. He built the new city of Angkor Thom on the site of the old capital, with the Bayon as its mystical and geographic center housing his royal essence. Instead of using the customary wooden ramparts to stop future aggressors, he built more than twenty-two miles of massive stone walls around the city. In addition to Angkor Thom, which includes the Bayon and the Royal Terraces, some of Jayavarman VII's most important monuments were Ta Prohm, Preah Khan, Neak Pean, Ta Som, and Sras Srang.

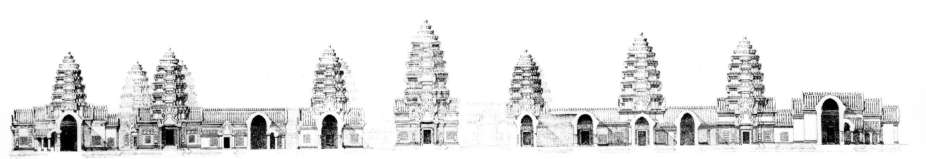

*Elevation of Ta Prohm. Drawn by Louis Delaporte and published in his folio* Monuments du Cambodge *in 1914*

Throughout the empire he built many facilities to serve the public needs, such as 102 hospitals, a great road system with 121 travelers' rest houses, and many monasteries. He also restored and enlarged the vast network of waterways.

An ardent Buddhist, Jayavarman VII followed the doctrines of the Mahāyāna school, which emphasizes salvation leading to a place in the western paradise with the help of the grace-giving Lokeshvara, the dispenser of compassion. It may well have been his desire to outshine the preceding Hindu dynasties and to spread his faith that spurred him to undertake so many projects.

The earliest of Jayavarman VII's major monuments, Ta Prohm, was dedicated to the king's mother, who, in accordance with the traditional Khmer practice of uniting the king's forebears with the gods after death, was given the form of Prajñāpāramita, a Buddhist goddess of wisdom. Within Ta Prohm there were also 260 other pious images, including one dedicated to the Brahman priest who had been the king's spiritual master. Besides being a monument to the dead queen, Ta Prohm functioned as a monastery supported by 3,000 villages and almost 80,000 people, some of whom were priests, officials, and dancers. This information is listed on an inscribed stone tablet in Ta Prohm, which also mentions treasures owned by the monastery, including golden dishes weighing some 1,100 lbs., silks from China, jewels, and many other precious objects.

Preah Khan was dedicated to Jayavarman VII's father, regarded as an incarnation of Lokeshvara. Both Preah Khan and Ta Prohm were built within the traditional four enclosures and display ceremonial gateways, moats and *barays,* sanctum towers, and covered terraces. The five-tower plan of Angkor Wat was abandoned for a more rectangular organization. The sanctuaries were built on low platforms; although much larger and more elaborate, these monuments are related in concept to Preah Ko and Lolei, which also had been dedicated to the parents and grandparents of the kings who built them. However, because chapels, annexes, and gateways were added to Preah Khan and Ta Prohm during the forty years of Jayavarman VII's reign, the final arrangement of both temples was confused.

Angkor Thom, which means large city, was Jayavarman VII's capital.

*Elevation of Preah Khan. Drawn by Louis Delaporte and published in* Monuments du Cambodge *in 1914*

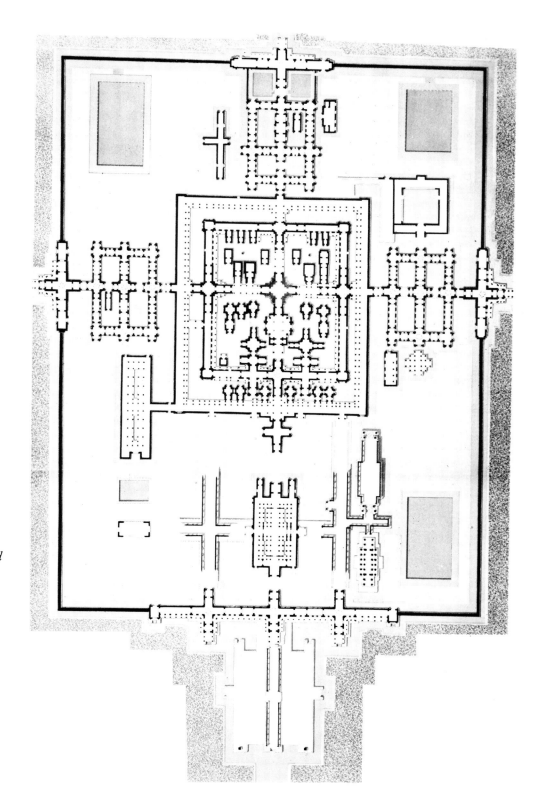

*Plan of Preah Khan. Drawn by Louis Delaporte and published in* Monuments du Cambodge *in 1914*

Four great gateways in the city wall, facing north, south, east, and west, lead to the Bayon at the city's geometric center. A fifth, the Gate of Victory, leads from the royal palace, built within the Phimeanakas enclosures, to the Eastern Baray. Each tower gateway has four giant faces of Lokeshvara, one facing in each direction.

Bridges over the moat that surrounds the city wall are lined with giant sculptures of the gods of heaven on one side and the demons of the underworld on the other, each of whom holds a section of a great snake. While, as already suggested, this may be the *nāga* bridge connecting the secular outer world and the sacred city of Angkor Thom, it may also be a dramatic, larger-than-life-size representation of the churning of the ocean which was said to have occurred during the creation of the world. According to the scriptures, in the previous dissolution of the world thirteen precious things had been lost. Among them were the sun, the moon, the goddess of beauty, the god of liquor, the heavenly physician, and the narrow-necked jar containing the elixir of immortality. Vishnu assumed the form of a tortoise, and the gods and demons broke off the peak of Mt. Mandara, the pillar that supports the heavens, and turned it upside down, using it as a churning rod on the back of the great tortoise. The serpent Sesha who lives in the cosmic ocean offered himself as a rope to twirl the churning stick. The gods took one end and the demons the other, and they churned for a thousand years until the lost items had been recovered.

Angkor Thom incorporates within its walls a number of earlier buildings, including the Baphuon and Phimeanakas. But its religious center is the Bayon, dedicated to the Buddha, with whom Jayavarman VII associated himself. The king carried on the god-king cult, and it seems likely that he substituted a Buddha image, the *Buddharāja,* for the *devarāja.*

Since the Bayon was built within Angkor Thom, its outer walls were omitted. Two rectangular covered terraces surround the center. The outer terrace has low reliefs dealing with the world of men, rather than with myths as in previous temples; the reliefs depict in specific detail the Cham-Khmer war and everyday life at Angkor. The low reliefs on the inner terrace show events concerning the gods. Lintels, door-jambs, and other architectural members are covered with such familiar motifs as heavenly maidens and dancers. The quality of carving ranges from brilliant to inferior and is unfinished in places, reflecting the enormous demands placed on the sculptors because of the vast numbers of buildings being worked on at the same time.

The center of the Bayon is awesome. It is a mass of crowded towers, each with four giant faces of Lokeshvara gazing down compassionately. In Lokeshvara's extended role as the Universal Buddha these smiling faces, looking in every direction at once, communicate the omnipresence of the supreme being. Unlike the towers at Angkor Wat, which still function architecturally to enclose space, the Bayon towers are boldly and frankly sculptural. Moreover, in contrast with the architectural clarity and harmony of Angkor Wat, the plan of the Bayon is crowded and unclear, partly because in several periods of his reign Jayavarman VII changed, rebuilt, and enlarged the Bayon as well as other buildings.

North of the Bayon, the long rectangular plaza bounded by the Royal Terraces on the west side was the social and temporal center of Angkor Thom. On top of the stone Elephant Terrace stood wooden pavilions decorated with gold, which sheltered the king and his court as they sat there to hold audiences and to view games, martial displays, or fireworks.

*Plan of the Bayon. Drawn by Louis Delaporte and published in* Monuments du Cambodge *in 1914*

Chou Ta-kuan, writing seventy-five years after the death of Jayavarman VII, described a royal audience: "The King holds an audience twice a day for the affairs of state. Officials and ordinary people who want to see him must sit on the ground and wait for him to appear. Distant music can be heard from the direction of the palace, conch shells herald his approach. I have heard that he is carried in a palanquin of gold. Then, the delicate fingers of two young women of the palace raise the curtain, revealing the king, sword in hand, sitting in the golden window. Ministers and citizens clasp their hands and touch their heads to the ground, raising themselves after the music ends. The king sits on the hereditary royal lion skin. When the audience ends, the attendants close the curtain."[12]

According to an inscription, Jayavarman VII "felt the affliction of his subjects more than his own because the suffering of the people constitutes

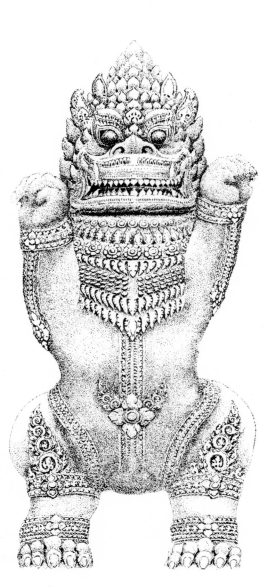

*Lion. Drawn by Louis Delaporte and published in* Monuments du Cambodge *in 1914*

*Nāga and garuda combined on a balustrade end. Drawn by Louis Delaporte and published in* Voyage au Cambodge *in 1880*

the suffering of the king, more than his own suffering."[13] Not only have some actual sculptured portraits from life of Jayavarman VII been identified; the faces of Lokeshvara as well may represent the king in his divine manifestation. Thus the king perpetuated the fusion of divine and royal power, following the form of the preceding Hindu monarchs, although the Buddha replaced Shiva or Vishnu as supreme deity. The king's omnipresent visage along with his restlessly aggrandizing building program have led some scholars to speculate that Jayavarman VII was a megalomaniac rather than the selfless paragon of piety described in the inscriptions.

Whatever his attitude toward his subjects may have been, Jayavarman VII's reign was the last burst of glory in the Angkor period. Vast human resources had been required to build and maintain the waterworks, construct the buildings, and carry on wars. Labor was supplied through a state system of conscription, supplemented by captured prisoners of war and indigenous mountain savages, who were purchased and used for domestic work. Succeeding kings were not able to command the power necessary to maintain this highly centralized theocracy and its extended empire. Many factors contributed to its decline. The neighboring Thai principalities, pressed by the Chinese, developed their armies and won back much of the northern and western sections of the Khmer Empire. The Khmer military failures cut off the supply of labor that had been provided by prisoners of war. Perhaps the citizens were exhausted by the demands of the god-king, the heavy tax burdens, the massive building programs, and the lengthy foreign wars, and welcomed the invaders as liberators from these obligations. The Thai armies brought the school of Hīnayāna Buddhism, which appealed to the masses with a doctrine of self-salvation that subverted both the necessity and the authority of the god-king.

In the ninth century, the site of Angkor had been desirable; now, with the new shift of power in the states to the north and west, the capital was exposed to constant harassment. A series of invasions weakened the central authority of the Khmer kings so that they could not maintain the massive and elaborate water system, which was frequently disrupted and polluted with the bodies of the victims of war. The unwatered rice fields reverted to an inhospitable jungle plain and the foul water made the inhabitants sick. In the middle of the fifteenth century the Khmer king finally abandoned Angkor, retreating south and east, away from the marauding Thais. The new capital of Phnom Penh was built at the confluence of the Mekong and Tonle Sap Rivers, and the brilliant period of Angkor's history ended.

*The jungle at the south gate to Angkor Thom, where a row of gods hold a great snake. Drawn by E. Tournois after a Delaporte drawing, and published in Garnier's* Voyages d'Exploration en Indo-Chine

# Ta Prohm

Ta Prohm was the first monument dedicated by Jayavarman VII, the last but most ambitious builder of the Angkor period. The king, a fervent Buddhist, built this complex to serve both as a shrine for his mother in the form of the Buddhist goddess of wisdom, Prajñāparāmita, and as a monastery. It lies just south of the southwest corner of the Eastern Baray.

85. *Ta Prohm, vines encircling the tower. 1186.*
*Sandstone*

Not only has this monument not been reconstructed, it has not even been freed of the strangling jungle growth. Countless visitors have recorded a unique feeling at seeing Angkor, and while this is surely due mostly to the exceptional qualities of the monuments themselves, there is also a kind of romantic excitement in seeing the ruins within their tangled green cover.

86. *Ta Prohm, a tree on top of a building. 1186. Sandstone*

A stone inscription found within the ruined sanctuary describes the king's spiritual goals. It says that he carries a sword that destroys the jungle of the passions on his course to supreme enlightenment, which is the understanding of ultimate reality. He upholds law honored in "three worlds," finding " 'satisfaction in the nectar, which is the religion of Sakyamuni,' Buddhism of the Greater Vehicle."[14]

# Preah Khan

87. *Preah Khan, entrance with guardians. 1191. Sandstone*

Preah Khan is north of the central city of Angkor Thom. It is a vast complex, the size of a city itself. Like Ta Prohm, it served a double function, as a shrine for the king's father in the form of Lokeshvara, and as a monastery with a hospital and rest house for travelers. As in many of Jayavarman VII's buildings, two large, freestanding guardians flank the gateways.

88. *Preah Khan, wall carving within the central enclosure. 1191. Sandstone*

At several periods, the king added more buildings to Preah Khan and other complexes, restlessly enlarging his tangible offerings in the service of the Buddhist faith. The carved walls are decorated with figures in the Buddhist pantheon. This row of cross-legged Buddhas sit inside flame-encircled niches beneath a vision of the luxuriant forests of paradise.

89. *Preah Khan, stone inscription. 1191. Sandstone*

This is one of some nine hundred stone inscriptions found in Indochina that give information about Angkor history. It is written in Sanskrit, the classical Indian language which introduced the written word into Cambodia around the time of Christ. Sanskrit continued to be used for inscriptions until the latter part of the fourteenth century.

90. *Preah Khan, building on columns. 1191. Sandstone*

Of Preah Khan's many buildings, this one is unique in form. The sanctuary rests on columns but there is no access stairway. It was probably modeled after contemporaneous wooden pavilions and had a wooden ladder or stair.

# Neak Pean

91. *Neak Pean, stone wall enclosing pool within dried-up baray.*
*Late 12th–early 13th century. Sandstone*

North of the Eastern Baray, an artificial lake five miles long, a smaller *baray* was built in conjunction with Preah Khan to provide water for the inhabitants of that vast temple complex. Neak Pean was built on a small circular island surrounded by a square pool within the *baray* of Preah Khan.

92. *Neak Pean, Lokeshvara carved on false door of sanctuary. Late 12th–early 13th century. Sandstone*

In the middle of the reservoir of Preah Khan, Neak Pean was built on what the inscription from Ta Prohm describes as "an eminent island, whose charm lies in its surrounding ponds which cleanse the soil of sins from those who visit it."[15] Its main pool, enclosed by a stone wall, was supposed to represent a legendary Buddhist lake in the Himalayas, Anavatāpta, whose waters possessed great curative powers. This pool fed four fountains, which spilled into smaller pools and represented the four great rivers of the world. The waters were used for ceremonial purposes and for cultivation—no drop was wasted.

93. *Neak Pean, the bodhisattva in the form of a horse saving shipwreck victims. Late 12th–early 13th century (reconstructed). Sandstone*

The compassionate *bodhisattva* who so often takes the form of Lokeshvara is shown here as a life-saving horse. Shipwreck victims cling to his sides as he guides them to safety. During the Angkor period, when the waterways and reservoirs were carefully maintained, water surrounded the image.

# Ta Som

94. *Ta Som, tower entrance. Late 12th–early 13th century. Sandstone*

Ta Som is at the east end of Preah Khan's *baray*. It is one of the temples related to the city-like establishment of Preah Khan that lies beyond its walls. A religious and administrative center, Preah Khan was given several thousand villages housing tens of thousands of people to supervise. The villagers provided revenues and food.

*95. Ta Som, gateway entrance. Late 12th–early 13th century. Sandstone*

The king dedicated Ta Som to his grandfather. Like Jayavarman VII's other monuments, it has entrance towers carved with the four faces of Lokeshvara looking north, south, east, and west. His gaze is a reflection of his capacity to be all-knowing and all-seeing.

96. *Ta Som, Lokeshvara's face on tower. Late 12th–early 13th century. Sandstone*

Today, green leaves crown the four faces of Lokeshvara on the gateway tower. Airborne seeds have rooted themselves and ruthlessly pried apart the stones. To keep up with the many constructions of Jayavarman VII, his craftsmen-builders fitted the stones together in haste, and as a result, none of his monuments has survived as well as earlier ones.

# Sras Srang

97. *Sras Srang, terrace overlooking the baray. Late 12th–early 13th century. Sandstone*

Sras Srang, one of the few *barays* still full of water, lies east of Banteay Kdei. It appears to be a natural lake which was paved and had its sides regularized by embankments. The terrace platform overlooking the water once held a wooden pavilion. Along the terrace are balustrades that curl up into *nāga* heads fancifully combined with *garudas*.

# Angkor Thom

98. *Angkor Thom, south bridge and gateway, distant view. Late 12th–early 13th century. Sandstone*

Five gateways afford access to Jayavarman VII's great walled city of Angkor Thom. Over the moat surrounding the city wall, a bridge lined with giant sculptures leads to each gate. There are images of the gods on one side of the roadway and demons on the other side, all holding part of two great *nāgas*.

99. *Angkor Thom, approach to south gateway: the gods. Late 12th–early 13th century. Sandstone*

The two great *nāgas* held by the giants may represent a double rainbow bridging heaven (here, the sacred city) and earth. The gateway arrangement also dramatizes a creation story told in Indian scriptures, the churning of the cosmic ocean.

100. *Angkor Thom, approach to south gateway: the demons. Late 12th–early 13th century. Sandstone*

In a previous dissolution of the world, the moon and the elixir of immortality were among the thirteen precious things lost. The gods and demons decided to churn the cosmic ocean in search of the missing treasures; they broke off the peak of Mt. Mandara, the pillar that supports the heavens, and turned it upside down to use as a churning rod. Vishnu, in the form of a tortoise, offered his back as the base for the churn.

101. *Angkor Thom, approach to south gateway: the demons. Late 12th–early 13th century. Sandstone*

The serpent Sesha, who lives in the cosmic ocean, offered himself as a rope to the gods and demons to twirl the churning stick. The gods took one end and the demons the other, and they churned for a thousand years until the lost items, including the elixir of immortality, had been recovered. The demons are distinguished by their round eyes, puffy cheeks, and fiercely animated brows and mouths, while the gods have almond eyes, smooth facial planes, and expressions of stern concentration.

102. *Angkor Thom, south gateway. Late 12th–
early 13th century. Sandstone*

The walls surrounding Angkor Thom are about two miles long on each
side. The enclosing wall is cut by five gateway towers, each of which has
faces similar to those found on the Bayon, though on a smaller scale.
The corbeled arch passageway is flanked by three fully rounded elephant
heads. Elephant traffic determined the height of the gateway.

# The Bayon

103. *The Bayon, distant view. Late 12th–early 13th century. Sandstone*

The Bayon, situated at the geographical center of Angkor Thom, is also its religious center. It lies a little to the southeast of Baphuon and Phime-anakas, each of which had served as the religious center for earlier Angkor cities on essentially the same site. Angkor Thom's city walls function as the outermost enclosure of the Bayon; its center is surrounded only by two sets of galleries.

104. *The Bayon, general view. Late 12th–early 13th century. Sandstone*

This vast pyramid temple contrasts sharply with its predecessors. Its plan is crowded—there are more than 50 towers—and confusing, partly because in several periods of his reign Jayavarman VII changed, rebuilt, and enlarged it as well as his other buildings. No one will really know how many times the Bayon was actually changed until the temple is taken apart. It seems that the first temple had a traditional rectangular plan. The subsequent changes were built on top of this foundation. The final form of the sanctum had a circular center to contain the *Buddharāja,* Jayavarman VII's divine manifestation. Twelve subsidiary chapels circled the center, housing images of deified regional governors.

105. *The Bayon. Late 12th–early 13th century.
Sandstone*

When the French scholars from the École Française d'Extrême-Orient
began to try to deduce the chronology of the various Angkor buildings,
the misreading of crucial inscriptions and the badly decayed state of the
Bayon led them to believe that the Bayon had been built in the eleventh
century. Because of the better state of preservation of Angkor Wat, they
believed that it, not the Bayon, was the last great Khmer monument.
When the inscriptions were reread and evaluated and the Bayon was
identified as a building of Jayavarman VII's reign, its poor condition was
attributed to hasty construction and subsequent vandalism by enemies
of the Buddhist faith, conquerors, and thieves.

106. *A Bayon tower, face of Lokeshvara. Late 12th–early 13th century. Sandstone*

The almond eyes, broad brow and cheeks, and wide nose of Lokeshvara are characteristic Khmer facial features. The expression of the full lips that curl up at the ends of the mouth is called "the smile of Angkor."

107. *The Bayon towers. Late 12th–early 13th century. Sandstone*

The center of the Bayon is circular, with a mass of crowded towers surrounding the central tower. The four smiling faces carved on every tower communicate the omnipresence of the supreme being.

There are many theories about specific human identity of the face towers. It has been suggested that the faces represented the king as Lokeshvara, the universal monarch. Another theory suggests that these faces represented regional governmental officials. If the latter theory is correct, it offers further evidence of the attempt to unite the entire population in the common cause of glorifying the god-king—a wish that may also have motivated the change to the mundane theme in the decorative reliefs of the Bayon's outer gallery from the world of gods to that of men.

108. *A Bayon tower, face of Lokeshvara.
Late 12th–early 13th century.
Sandstone*

Lokeshvara wears the crown and jewels customary for *bodhisattva* images all over Asia. However, in accord with the Khmer facial features, he wears jewelry fashioned in keeping with the Angkor styles. The unusual necklace of lotus rosettes exemplifies the Angkor idea of celestial jewelry.

109. *The Bayon, carved pillar. Late 12th–early 13th century. Sandstone*

Two celestial beings dance on top of lotus flowers. Their hands and feet communicate the message of their dance, suspended timelessly in stone. Court dancers entertained Jayavarman VII with this kind of dance; classical dancers in Cambodia and Thailand still perform in the same style.

110. *The Bayon, carved pillar. Late 12th–early 13th century. Sandstone*

A group of three dancers performs on lotus flowers within a serpentine niche. Unlike the *tevodas*, the dancers wear short skirts. A pattern of flame and foliage in low relief covers the stone above the niche.

111. *The Bayon, view through the outer gallery to the inner gallery and center. Late 12th–early 13th century. Sandstone*

The sacred temple-mountain is dramatically framed by a doorway of the outer gallery. A wealth of knowledge about the techniques of war in the twelfth century is carved into the outer gallery wall. These reliefs tell the story of the struggles between the Cham and Khmer kingdoms; they also show peaceful days at Angkor, in charming vignettes of daily life. Such scenes of ordinary people and ordinary life mark a radical departure in theme from the decoration of earlier temples, which had been concerned only with divine and royal figures.

112. *The Bayon, outer terrace. Late 12th–early 13th century. Sandstone*

Originally the outer gallery was covered by a roof, supported by the wall on one side and columns on the other. The pilgrim could walk around the sanctum, protected from the hot sun or monsoon rains, and see the stories of Khmer history and the gods carved on the walls while paying homage to the god-king.

113. *The Bayon, bas-relief of Cham-Khmer war, from the outer terrace. Late 12th–early 13th century. Sandstone*

The great bas-relief along the outer gallery is divided into three rows; here the story of the long struggle between the Chams and the Khmers is told. The Chams invaded and sacked Angkor in 1177. After many battles, Jayavarman defeated the Chams, installing himself as king in 1181. In this simultaneous narrative style, warriors riding elephants fight on the top row as foot soldiers struggle in another battle scene in the central register; meanwhile, a naval battle takes place below.

114. *Detail of Plate 113.* The naval battle is being fought from a long boat resembling an oversized canoe. The position of the spear-carrying warriors with their wing-like shields above the seated oarsmen is meant to indicate that the warriors are behind the oarsmen; this is the only sign of depth in space. The water is suggested by the fish swimming beside and below the boat, among floating corpses of soldiers.

115. *The Bayon, bas-relief of Cham-Khmer war, from the outer terrace. Late 12th–early 13th century. Sandstone*

A great war boat carries spear-bearing warriors into another battle. The bodies of warriors float beside the boat. Below, a row of vignettes shows life on land; a musician and some people drink wine under a thatched roof on the far right, and others on the left hunt in the jungle for game.

116. *Detail of plate 115*

This close-up view shows the faces of grimacing Cham warriors in profile, and their shoulders turned squarely forward. They are distinguishable from the Khmers by their helmets, which look like lotus flowers turned upside down. The warrior steering the boat sits at the right; helmeted rowers sit below the standing warriors, protected from enemy spears by a single long, woven shield, the texture of which has been carefully etched into the stone.

117. *The Bayon, bas-relief of Cham-Khmer war, from the outer terrace. Late 12th–early 13th century. Sandstone*

Two war boats float in waters rich with fish. The boat on the left is decorated with the head of an open-mouthed *makara* sticking out his flame-like tongue; below the other boat, a crocodile and a goose have caught themselves a fish dinner. In a narrative style of swiftly changing scenes, the lower register contains a jungle scene with a group of cranes on the left, a man killing a small animal in the center, some monkeys, a tiger eating a man, and some people taking their goods to market on the right.

118. *The Bayon, bas-relief of Cham-Khmer war, from the outer terrace. Late 12th–early 13th century. Sandstone*

The *makara* face on the Khmer war boat in the center is very much like the faces on the "dragon boats" still raced at festival time on both the Mekong River in Cambodia and the Menam River in Thailand. Above the naval scene a male acrobat, shown in a fully frontal position, holds his foot in his hand; he performs for a group of men on either side, who are depicted with faces and legs in profile and squarely frontal shoulders. At the bottom, under thatched pavilions, Khmers shown in profile eat and gossip while fire-tenders sit in the open air in the center.

119. *The Bayon, bas-relief depicting scenes from daily life, from the outer terrace. Late 12th–early 13th century. Sandstone*

In the center of the left side of these scenes of daily life, an old man being comforted by a younger man sits in an elaborately decorated wood and thatch pavilion that gives us a good picture of the secular architecture that has disappeared from Angkor Thom. At the top center, the anchor of a deep-hulled ship is being weighed while the woven reed sails are being hoisted; two men play chess in the bow. Below the ship, two small canoes hold fishermen who have just cast their nets, which look like canopies for the raucous shipboard party going on in another boat below them. The bottom row shows city scenes: on the left, a woman on a dais surrounded by other women and a child; on the right, a man carrying goods to market, an old woman reading a palm, a shop selling rice, and, on the far right, a cockfight.

# Royal Terraces

120. *Angkor Thom, Elephant Terrace, south end of Royal Terrace.
Late 12th–early 13th century. Sandstone*

The Royal Terrace lies in front of the Phimeanakas enclosure facing a
great open space in the shape of an elongated rectangle. This open space—
the main square of Angkor Thom—was the secular center of the city.
Angkor Thom's fifth gate, the Gate of Victory, gives direct access from
outside the city to the great square, by way of an old axial roadway
leading from the Eastern Baray.

121. *Angkor Thom, Elephant Terrace. Late 12th–early 13th century. Sandstone*

Wooden pavilions decorated with gold once stood on top of the stone Elephant Terrace. The carved relief of stately elephants suggests the grand style of the displays the king and his court must have witnessed from the pavilions.

122. *Angkor Thom, Elephant Terrace. Late 12th–early 13th century. Sandstone*

The hunt appears to be the theme of this great procession of elephants; the noble hunter sits in a saddle with the driver mounted on the beast's neck. Three stairways project into the square; this one has fully rounded elephant heads, plucking lotuses with their trunks, at the corner.

123. *Angkor Thom, central section of Royal Terrace with lions and garudas. Late 12th–early 13th century. Sandstone*

Projecting into the square, three elephant heads come into view on the side of the central staircase. The north section of the terrace is decorated with relief carvings of lions and *garudas*. Both the lion, which is not native to the Cambodian jungle, and the *garuda,* which is mythical, have royal and religious associations.

124. *Angkor Thom, central section of the Royal Terrace with lions and garudas. Late 12th–early 13th century. Sandstone*

According to the myths, the gods lived in "flying palaces" which moved about the cosmos at the whim of the celestials. These lions and *garudas* are shown performing their mission of carrying the palace through the air, a clear reference to the fact that the royal palace was a copy of the celestial prototype.

125. *Angkor Thom, lions and garudas within the Royal Terrace. Late 12th–early 13th century. Sandstone*

At some point or other during his reign, Jayavarman VII apparently changed and enlarged all his monuments. The Royal Terrace was no exception. At one time these lions and *garudas* decoratively upheld the wood pavilions above; then the enlarged terrace covered over the old outside wall. Remnants of the balustrades with their combined *nāga-garuda* heads can be seen in the distance.

126. *Angkor Thom, five-headed horse, Royal Terrace. Late 12th–early 13th century. Sandstone.*

The compassionate *bodhisattva,* widely worshiped in Jayavarman VII's time, is shown here as a five-headed horse. This carving, like the lions and *garudas* in Plate 125, was walled in on two sides during an enlargement of the terrace; however, it is still accessible on one side. Beside the horse, jeweled dancers, surrounded by a host of admirers, perform on lotus flowers.

127. *Angkor Thom, five-headed horse, Royal Terrace. Late 12th–early 13th century. Sandstone*

The powerful chest of the five-headed horse, who represents the *bodhisattva,* is covered with bands of jewels. His heads are all crowned, his manes neatly combed, and lotus rosettes adorn his foreheads. Pious figures shown in profile kneel on lotuses at either side.

128. *Angkor Thom, stairway to Royal Terrace. Late 12th–early 13th century. Sandstone*

The architectural components, such as ceremonial stairs, causeways, and terraces, used throughout the Angkor complexes are somewhat lacking in variety. However, one must try to remember that these stone creations furnished the background for lavish pageantry. Graceful dancers decorated with shimmering jewels performed on the terraces, and a host of officials wearing skirts woven with gorgeous combinations of colored and metallic threads ascended the stairs in stately processions.

129. *Angkor Thom, lion, Royal Terrace. Late 12th–early 13th century. Sandstone*

Marauders would not fear this lion with every curl neatly in place; instead of muscular tension, his body expresses a ponderous rigidity. The proverbial lion-guardian of the stairs has royal associations—king of the beasts as guardian for the king of men. In his formal role in Buddhism, the Buddha is called the lion of the church, and when the Buddha speaks, it is said that his voice sounds like the roar of a lion.

130. *Angkor Thom, the "Leper King." Late 12th–early 13th century. Sandstone*

North of the Royal Terrace lies the Terrace of the "Leper King." Popular legend thus named the seated figure on the top of the terrace, which may originally have been installed in another site. Unlike most Khmer images, the figure is sexless; it wears no crown to suggest kingship, and, while leprosy was prevalent in Angkor, its association with this image probably comes from the mold and fungus growing on the stone.

131. *Angkor Thom, Terrace of the "Leper King."*
*Late 12th–early 13th century. Sandstone*

The Terrace of the "Leper King" may have been the cremation site for the royal family and important officials. During reconstruction, a second wall was uncovered behind the first. It is thought that the second wall was covered not in a remodeling or an expansion of the terrace, but rather, as soon as it was built. Since the figures carved on the covered wall represent the demons of the underworld, it probably symbolizes the lower depths, beneath the earth's surface.

132. *Angkor Thom, detail of relief, Terrace of the "Leper King."*
*Late 12th–early 13th century. Sandstone*

In a close-up view of the carved walls, one can see rows of male and
female figures wearing crowns and carrying lotus flowers. The figures
do not appear to be divine beings; they may be spirits of the earth.

133. *Angkor Thom, Terrace of the "Leper King."*
*Late 12th–early 13th century (under reconstruction).*
*Sandstone*

Reconstruction of this terrace was underway in 1970 before the Cambodian civil war broke out. The stones from the outer wall have been carried away to rebuild the interior. A few demon faces from the intentionally covered wall can be seen at the bottom where the outer wall ends.

134. *Angkor Thom, Sras Srei. Late 12th–early 13th century. Sandstone*

Sras Srei—the "women's bath" in the Khmer language—lies within the royal enclosure of the walls of Phimeanakas. Chou Ta-kuan tells us that the country was terribly hot day and night, and that one often bathed several times a day. Perhaps this pool was used exclusively by the palace women; however, he reports seeing mixed bathing practiced without shame: "to enter the water, the women simply hide their sex with their left hands."[16]

*135. Angkor Thom, south gateway approach. Late 12th–early 13th century. Sandstone*

Upon leaving Jayavarman VII's city of Angkor Thom, the visitor once more passes through one of the five gateways. The giant gods and demons are seen pulling the serpent Sesha to twirl the churning rod, commemorating the churning of the ocean when they recovered the elixir of immortality.

# NOTES

1. George Coedès, *The Indianized States of Southeast Asia* (Honolulu: East-West Center Press, 1968), p. 111.

2. *Ibid.,* p. 115.

3. *Ibid.,* p. 116.

4. Paul Pelliot, *Mémoires sur les coutumes du Cambodge de Tcheou Ta-kouan* (Paris: A. Maisonneuve, 1951), p. 11.

5. *Ibid.,* p. 12.

6. Coedès, *op. cit.,* p. 159.

7. Pierre Loti, *Un Pèlerin d'Angkor* (Paris: Calmann-Lévy, 1912), p. 77.

8. Pelliot, *op. cit.,* p. 33.

9. George Coedès, *Angkor* (New York and Hong Kong: Oxford University Press, 1963), p. 87.

10. *Ibid.*

11. *Ibid.,* p. 88.

12. Pelliot, *op. cit.,* p. 35.

13. Coedès, *Angkor, op. cit.,* p. 104.

14. *Ibid.,* p. 95.

15. *Ibid.,* p. 97.

16. Pelliot, *op. cit.,* p. 33.

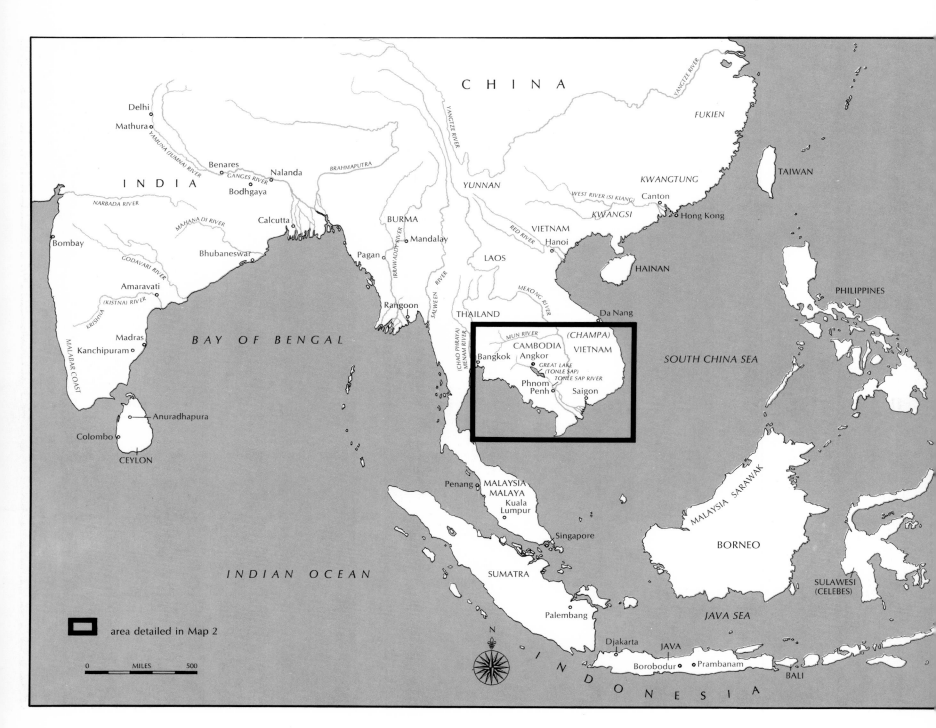

*Map 1. Southeast Asia*

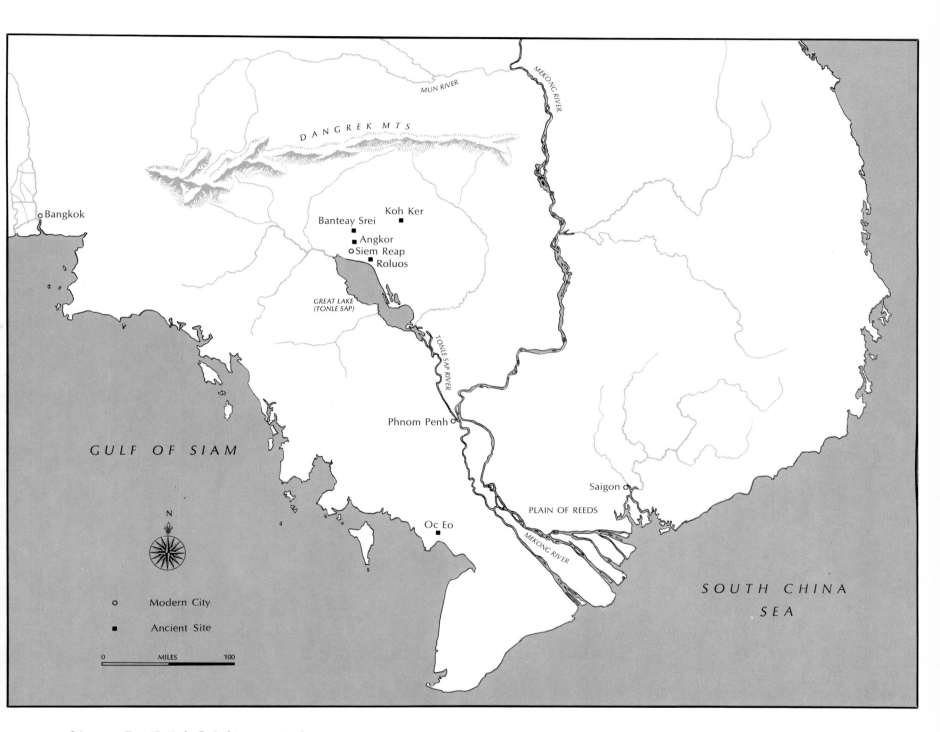

MUN RIVER

MEKONG RIVER

DANGREK MTS

Bangkok

Koh Ker

Banteay Srei

Angkor

Siem Reap

Roluos

GREAT LAKE
(TONLE SAP)

TONLE SAP RIVER

Phnom Penh

GULF OF SIAM

Saigon

PLAIN OF REEDS

N

Oc Eo

MEKONG RIVER

SOUTH CHINA
SEA

o   Modern City

■   Ancient Site

0        MILES        100

Map 2.   Detail of the Indochinese peninsula

225

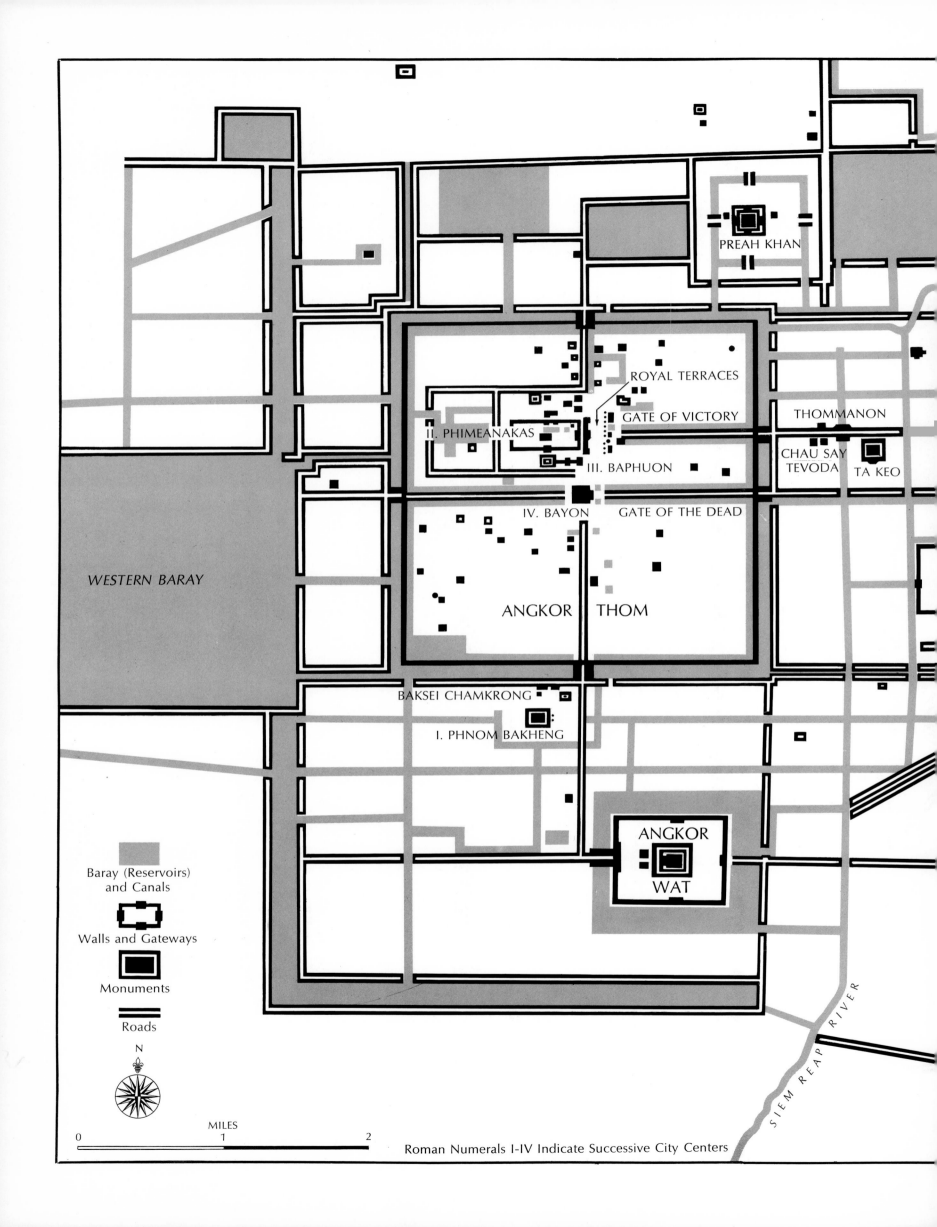

PREAH KHAN

ROYAL TERRACES

GATE OF VICTORY

THOMMANON

II. PHIMEANAKAS

CHAU SAY
TEVODA

TA KEO

III. BAPHUON

IV. BAYON

GATE OF THE DEAD

WESTERN BARAY

ANGKOR    THOM

BAKSEI CHAMKRONG

I. PHNOM BAKHENG

ANGKOR
WAT

Baray (Reservoirs)
and Canals

Walls and Gateways

Monuments

Roads

N

SIEM REAP RIVER

MILES

0                    1                    2

Roman Numerals I-IV Indicate Successive City Centers

# Plan of Angkor

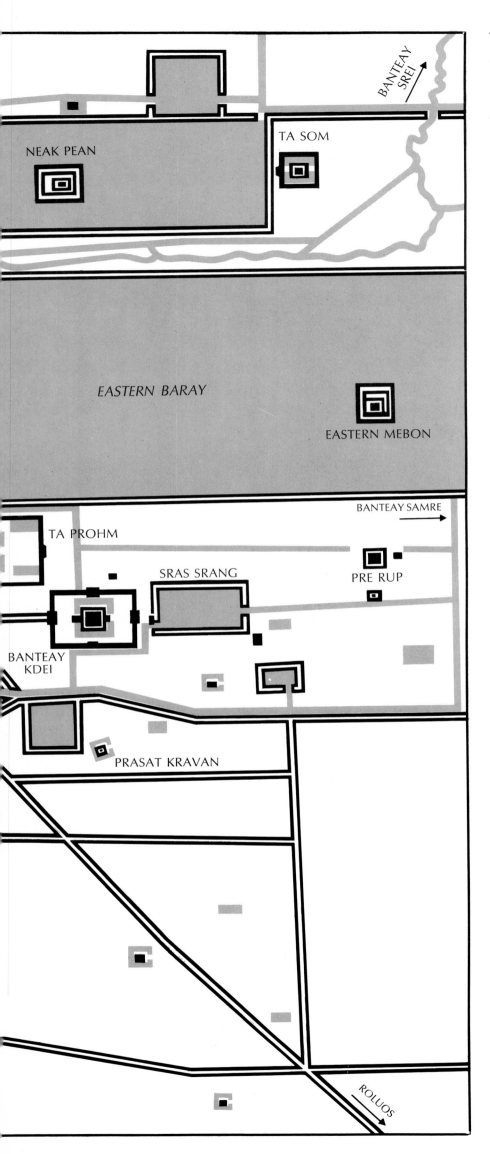

*Map 3.   Plan of the central part of the Angkor site*

# CHRONOLOGY OF ANCIENT CAMBODIA

| KINGS | REIGNS | SITE | MONUMENTS | HISTORICAL EVENTS |
|---|---|---|---|---|
| Kaundinya (legendary) | 1st century A.D. | Funan | | Kingdom of Funan: 1st–6th century A.D. |
| Kaundinya | c. 400–c. 420 | | | |
| Kaundinya Jayavarman | c. 478–514 | | | |
| Jayavarman I | 657–681 | | | Kingdoms of Chenla: 6th–8th century A.D. |
| Jayavarman II | 802–850 | | | Founding of empire at Angkor. Capital established at Roluos in Angkor region. Institution of god-king cult; royal patronage of Shiva |
| Jayavarman III | 850–877 | | | |
| Indravarman I | 877–889 | Roluos | Preah Ko 879<br>Baray Bakong 881 | |
| Yashovarman I | 889–900 | Roluos<br>Angkor | Lolei 893<br>Eastern Baray | New capital at Angkor, called Yashodharapura |
| Harshavarman I | 900–921? | Angkor | Prasat Kravan 921 | |
| Ishanavarman II | 921? | Angkor | Baksei Chamkrong | Struggle for succession; usurpation and removal of capital from Angkor to Koh Ker |
| Jayavarman IV | 921–941 | Koh Ker | | |
| Harshavarman II | 941–944 | | | |
| Rājendravarman | 944–968 | Angkor<br>Angkor<br>Banteay Srei | Eastern Mebon 952<br>Pre Rup 961<br>Banteay Srei 967 | Return to Angkor capital<br>Wars with Champa |
| Jayavarman V | 968–1001 | Angkor | Phimeanakas | Domination of Angkor over Siam and Malaya |
| Udayādityavarman I | 1001–1002 | | | |
| Sūryavarman I | 1002–1050 | Angkor | Ta Keo | Struggle for succession 1002–1011 |
| Udayādityavarman II | 1050–1066 | Angkor<br><br>Angkor | Baphuon, c. 1050–1066<br>Western Baray | Revolts 1051, 1064<br><br>Unsuccessful campaign against Champa |

| KINGS | REIGNS | SITE | MONUMENTS | HISTORICAL EVENTS |
|---|---|---|---|---|
| Harshavarman III | 1066–1080 | | | |
| Jayavarman VI | 1080–1107 | | | |
| Dharanindravarman I | 1107–1113 | | | |
| Sūryavarman II | 1113–after 1145 | Angkor | Thommanon | Struggle for succession |
| | | Angkor | Chau Say Tevoda | Royal patronage of Vishnu |
| | | Angkor | Angkor Wat | Domination of Siam, Malaya, Champa, and Laos |
| | | Angkor | Banteay Samre | |
| Dharanindravarman II | c. 1160 | | | |
| Yashovarman II | 1160–1165 | | | |
| Tribhuvanādityavarman | 1165–1177 | | | Chams sack Angkor 1177 |
| Jayavarman VII | 1181–c. 1220 | Angkor | Ta Prohm 1186 | Royal patronage of Mahāyāna |
| | | Angkor | Preah Khan 1191 | Buddhism |
| | | Angkor | Neak Pean | |
| | | Angkor | Ta Som | |
| | | Angkor | Sras Srang | |
| | | Angkor | Angkor Thom | |
| | | Angkor | Bayon | |
| | | Angkor | Royal Terraces | |
| | | Angkor | Sras Srei | Withdrawal from Champa 1220 |
| | | | | Decline of Khmer power |
| Indravarman II | d. 1243 | | | Rise of Thai principalities |
| Jayavarman VIII | 1243–1295 | | | Spread of Hīnayāna Buddhism and Islam in Southeast Asia |
| | | | | Mongol invasion repulsed 1282 |
| | | | | Chou Ta-kuan, Mongol envoy, at Angkor 1296 |
| | | | | Thai armies conquer Angkor 1353 |
| | | | | End of Sanskrit inscriptions |
| | | | | Thai armies recapture Angkor 1431 |
| | | | | Removal of capital to Phnom Penh |

*Note:* The kings listed represent most of the reigning monarchs who were associated with the monuments of Angkor illustrated in this book. The facts that the Khmer Empire went through a series of periods of divided authority and that genealogical information for Cambodia is incomplete are reflected in the lapses in this chronology.

# GLOSSARY

*Angkor*   From the Sanskrit *nagara,* royal city or capital. The Khmer capital from the tenth to fifteenth centuries. At least four successive cities were built on this site, the last of which was Angkor Thom at the end of the twelfth century

*Banteay*   Citadel

*Baray*   Reservoir

*Bodhisattva*   A compassionate being who could become a Buddha but elects to stay on earth to help all sentient beings to their enlightenment, aiding them toward rebirth in the Western Paradise

*Buddha*   Literally, a being who has attained enlightenment; historically, an Indian religious leader born in the sixth century B.C.

*Cham*   The people of Champa, the rival state adjoining Cambodia which is modern South Vietnam; its capital was Da Nang

*Deva*   A god

*Devarāja*   Literally, god-king; a phallus symbolizing the spiritual and royal essence of the Khmer king, his godlike aspect and his temporal power. Divinity was bestowed on the king by Shiva through the medium of a Brahman priest

*Garuda*   Mythical creature with the head of a bird and a human body, on which Vishnu rode

*Hīnayāna*   Literally, "Lesser Vehicle" in Sanskrit: a school of Buddhism that emphasizes self-salvation. Hīnayāna Buddhism, introduced to Indochina in the twelfth century, became the predominant religion in Cambodia in the fifteenth century, as it remains today

*Indra*   King of the early Hindu gods, and bringer of rain and storms

*Jaya*   Victory

*Kāla*   Mythical monster with a grinning face and bulging eyes; the lower jaw is absent below its protruding teeth

*Khmer*   The ancient indigenous people of Cambodia

*Ko*   Bull

*Krishna*   An avatar or incarnation of Vishnu

*Lingam*   Form of Shiva as a phallic symbol

*Lokeshvara*   Literally, "world-lord": name often used in Asia for the compassionate *bodhisattva* Avalokiteshvara. At the Bayon and on the other gateway towers built by Jayavarman VII, Lokeshvara assumes the role of the Universal Buddha, who represents the central force of creation in the universe

230

*Mahābhārata*  One of the great Indian epics, along with the *Ramāyana*

*Mahāyāna*  Literally, "Greater Vehicle" in Sanskrit: a school of Buddhism that emphasizes salvation from suffering not through self-discipline, but through the grace of numerous deities of the Buddhist pantheon. Mahāyāna Buddhism flourished in Cambodia from the first century until the middle of the thirteenth century

*Makara*  Mythical water monster which has the body of a crocodile and the trunk of an elephant

*Mt. Meru*  The mythical mountain sacred to Hindus and Buddhists, which is the center of the world and residence of the gods

*Nāga*  Snake god and mythical progenitor of the Khmer race

*Nandi*  Shiva's sacred bull

*Phnom*  Mountain

*Preah*  Sacred

*Rāja*  Ruler or king

*Rāma*  One of the avatars or incarnations of Vishnu and the hero of the *Rāmāyana*

*Rāmāyana*  An Indian epic which tells the story of Rāma and Sita

*Sita*  Rāma's wife and heroine of the *Rāmāyana*

*Shiva*  One of the two supreme Hindu gods. Shiva, creator and destroyer of the universe, was often worshiped in his phallic form, the *lingam*

*Sras*  Pond

*Srei*  Woman

*Stupa*  Perhaps originally an Indian funerary mound; adapted as a form for Buddhist monuments

*Sugriva*  King of the monkeys after he defeats his brother Vali. He is Rāma's ally in the *Rāmāyana*

*Sūrya*  The Hindu sun god

*Ta*  Ancestor

*Tevoda*  Divine female who inhabits the palaces of heaven

*Thom*  Large

*Varman*  The protected, protégé, the victorious

*Vishnu*  One of the two supreme Hindu gods. According to Indian scriptures, Vishnu, preserver of the universe, appears in ten forms or avatars to destroy the evil tyrants of the earth each time the world is re-created

*Wat*  Monastery

# LIST OF ILLUSTRATIONS

232

# BIBLIOGRAPHY

*Abbreviations for Periodicals*

*AA   Artibus Asiae,* Ascona, Switzerland

*BEFEO   Bulletin de l'École Française  d'Extrême-Orient,* Hanoi

*JA   Journal Asiatique,* Paris

*IAL   Indian Arts and Letters,* London


Auboyer, Jeannine. *L'Art Khmer au Musée Guimet.* Paris: Louvre, Publications du Service éducatif No. 7, 1956 (?).

Aymonier, Étienne. *Le Cambodge.* 3 vols. Paris: E. Leroux, 1900–1904.

Boisselier, Jean. *Le Cambodge.* Paris, 1966.

———. *La Statuaire Khmère et son Évolution.* Saigon: École Française d'Extrême-Orient, 1955.

———. *Tendances de l'art Khmer.* Paris: Presses universitaires, 1956.

Briggs, Lawrence Palmer. *The Ancient Khmer Empire.* Philadelphia: American Philosophical Society, 1951.

Coedès, George. *Angkor: An Introduction.* Translated and edited by Emily Floyd Gardiner. New York and Hong Kong: Oxford University Press, 1963. Translation of *Pour mieux comprendre Angkor.* 2nd ed. Paris: A. Maisonneuve, 1947.

———. Bibliography of Coedès' work, *AA,* XXIV, No. 3–4 (1961), 155.

———. "La Désignation funéraire des grands monuments Khmers," *BEFEO,* XL (1940), 315.

———. *The Indianized States of Southeast Asia.* Translated by Susan Brown Cowing. Honolulu: East-West Center Press, 1968. Translation of *Les États hindouisés d'Indochine et d'Indonésie.* Paris: De Boccard, 1963.

———. "La Stèle de Práh Khan d'Angkor," *BEFEO,* XLI (1941), 255.

Coral Remusat, Gilberte de. *L'Art Khmer: les grandes étapes de son évolution.* Paris: Les Éditions d'Art et d'Histoire, 1940.

Delaporte, Louis. *Les Monuments du Cambodge.* 2 vols. Paris: Commission Archéologique de l'Indochine, 1914–24.

———. *Voyage au Cambodge.* Paris: C. Delagrave, 1880.

Finot, Louis. "Notes d'épigraphie," *BEFEO,* I–XXXV (1901–35).

———, Goloubew, Victor, and Coedès, George. *Le Temple d'Angkor Vat.* 7 vols. Paris: Van Oest, 1927–32.

———, Marchal, Henri, and Parmentier, Henri. *Le Temple d'Içvarapura.* Paris: Van Oest, 1926.

Garnier, François. *Voyages d'exploration en Indo-Chine.* Paris: Hachette, 1873.

Ghosh, Manomoham. *A History of Cambodia.* Saigon: J. K. Gupta, 1960.

Giteau, Madeleine. *Khmer Sculpture and the Angkor Civilization.* New York: Harry N. Abrams, 1965.

GLAIZE, MAURICE. *Les Monuments du groupe d'Angkor; guide.* 3rd ed. Paris: A. Maisonneuve, 1963.

GOLOUBEW, VICTOR. "Le Cheval Balāha," *BEFEO,* XXVII (1927), 223.

GROSLIER, BERNARD-PHILIPPE. *Angkor et le Cambodge au XVI<sup>e</sup> siècle d'après les sources portugaises et espagnoles.* Paris: Presses universitaires, 1958.

———. *The Art of Indochina.* New York: Crown, 1962.

———, and ARTHAUD, JACQUES. *Angkor, Art and Civilization.* Rev. ed. New York: Praeger, 1966.

GROSLIER, GEORGES. *Recherches sur les cambodgiens.* Paris: A. Challamel, 1921.

HALL, D. G. E. *A History of South-East Asia.* 2nd ed. New York: St. Martin's Press; London: Macmillan, 1964.

LEE, SHERMAN. *Ancient Cambodian Sculpture.* New York: The Asia Society, 1969.

LOTI, PIERRE. *Un Pèlerin d'Angkor.* Paris: Calmann-Lévy, 1912.

MARCHAL, HENRI. *Les Temples d'Angkor.* 6th ed. Paris: A. Guillot, 1955.

MARTINI, FRANÇOIS. "En Marge du Ramayana cambodgien," *BEFEO,* XXXVIII (1938), 285, and *JA,* CCXXXVIII (1950), 81.

MA TOUAN-LIN. *Ethnographie des peuples étrangers à la Chine.* Translated by d'Hervey de Saint Denys. Geneva, 1876–83.

MONTGOMERY, GEORGE (ed.). *Khmer Sculpture.* New York: The Asia Society, 1961.

MORÓN, ELEANOR. "Angkor Wat: Meaning Through Measurements." Master's thesis. Ann Arbor: University of Michigan, 1974.

MUS, PAUL. "Angkor in the Time of Jayavarman VII," *IAL,* XI, No. 2 (1937), 65.

———. "Le Sourire d'Angkor," *AA,* XXIV, No. 3–4 (1961), 363.

PARMENTIER, HENRI. *L'Art khmer classique.* Paris: Les Éditions d'art et d'histoire, 1939.

PELLIOT, PAUL. *Mémoires sur les coutumes du Cambodge de Tcheou Ta-kouan.* Paris: A. Maisonneuve, 1951.

PYM, CHRISTOPHER. *The Ancient Civilization of Angkor.* New York: Mentor, 1968.

——— (ed.). *Henri Mouhot's Diary.* New York: Oxford University Press, 1966.

ROWLAND, BENJAMIN. *The Art and Architecture of India: Buddhist, Hindu, Jain.* Baltimore: Penguin, 1967.

SCHAFER, EDWARD H. *The Vermilion Bird: T'ang Images of the South.* Berkeley: University of California Press, 1967.

*The Srimad-Bhagavatam of Krishna-Dwaipayana Vyasa.* Translated from the original Sanskrit text by J. M. Sanyal. Calcutta: Oriental Pub. Co., n.d.

STERN, PHILIPPE. *Les Monuments khmers du style du Bayon et Jayavarman VII*. Paris: Presses universitaires, 1965.

TROUVÉ, G. M. "Travaux de sondages executés sous le dallage du sanctuaire central d'Angkor Vat," *BEFEO*, XXXV (1935), 483.

ZIMMER, HEINRICH. *Myths and Symbols in Indian Art*, ed. Joseph Campbell. New York: Pantheon, 1946.

# INDEX

239

76964

76964